Junior Science
Book 3

GALORE PARK

Junior Science
Book 3

Sue Hunter and Jenny Macdonald

Editor: David Penter
Series Editor: Louise Martine

www.galorepark.co.uk

Published by Galore Park Publishing Ltd
19/21 Sayers Lane, Tenterden, Kent TN30 6BW
www.galorepark.co.uk

Layout by Typetechnique
Technical illustrations by Ian Moores
Cartoon illustrations by Rowan Barnes-Murphy

Printed by Replika Press, India

ISBN: 978 1905735 32 7

First published 2010, reprinted 2011, 2012

To accompany this course:
Junior Science 3 Teacher's Resource
ISBN 978 1 905735 41 9 or available as a download

Details of other Galore Park publications are available at
www.galorepark.co.uk

ISEB Revision Guides, publications and examination papers may also be
obtained from Galore Park

About the authors

Sue Hunter has been a science teacher in a variety of schools for more years than she cares to remember. Her experiences have included teaching in a choir school and a London middle school, teaching GCSE and A level in the Netherlands and a short spell as a full-time mother of two. She is Head of Science at St Hugh's School in Oxfordshire and a member of the Common Entrance setting team. She has run a number of training courses for prep school teachers, including at Malvern College and for the Independent Association of Preparatory Schools (IAPS), and is currently IAPS Support Co-ordinator for science and a member of the Independent Schools Inspectorate.

Jenny Macdonald has been a teacher since graduating in 1973, teaching in both state and private schools, and for the last ten years has taught science to Years 3 to 6 at St Hugh's School in Oxfordshire. After marrying in the mid-1970s, she moved to Oxfordshire and in the 1980s the family acquired a smallholding where she raised three children before graduating to sheep, chickens, cats and dogs. She is a keen singer in several local choirs, enjoys outdoor pursuits and has travelled extensively, helping her husband undertake research work on wildlife conservation projects around the world.

Working safely

Suggestions for practical work in the 'To do' sections may involve potential hazards and these have been highlighted with the symbols ⚠ and 🛡. Guidance on how to conduct practical work safely within the classroom environment is given in the Teacher's Resource which accompanies this book.

Preface

The most exciting phrase to hear in science, the one that heralds new discoveries, is not 'Eureka!' but 'That's funny ...' **Isaac Asimov**

The study of science for young children is a voyage of discovery. It stimulates their curiosity and provides a vehicle for them to explore their world, to ask questions about things that they observe and to make sense of their observations. It does not exist in isolation but draws upon many other aspects of a well-rounded curriculum and should be practical, interesting and, above all, fun.

This book is the final of three Junior Science books designed to be used in Years 3 to 5. The three books together can be used to underpin a course of study leading to the 11+ Common Entrance examinations and link directly into *So You Really Want to Learn Science* Books 1 and 2, by Ron Pickering. The books are designed in such a way that they can be used as a course in their own right, one book for each of Years 3 to 5, or as a resource to support an existing scheme of work.

Acknowledgements

We are immensely grateful to Louise Martine and Terry Hardy for their support in preparing this book and to David Penter for casting his expert eye over the script.

Thanks must also go to our families for putting up with erratically-timed meals, producing cups of coffee and tea or glasses of wine at appropriate moments and providing support and encouragement throughout the gestation period of the book.

Lastly, we should thank the pupils at St Hugh's School, Carswell, for (unwittingly) acting as guinea pigs for much of the material in the book. Their unfailing enthusiasm for science has been our inspiration and this book is for them.

Sue Hunter and Jenny Macdonald
September 2010

Contents

Chapter 1: Life processes

Chapter 2: Adaptation and evolution

Chapter 3: Life cycles

Chapter 4: Healthy living

Chapter 5: Microbes

Chapter 6: Separating mixtures

Chapter 7: Chemical changes

Chapter 8: Soils

Chapter 9: Hear the sound

Chapter 10: More about forces

Chapter 1: Life processes

Alive or not?

In science we often try to group things according to their similarities. This helps us to think about them more clearly and understand them better.

Look at these pictures. Discuss with your partner or group how you could sort these things into groups.

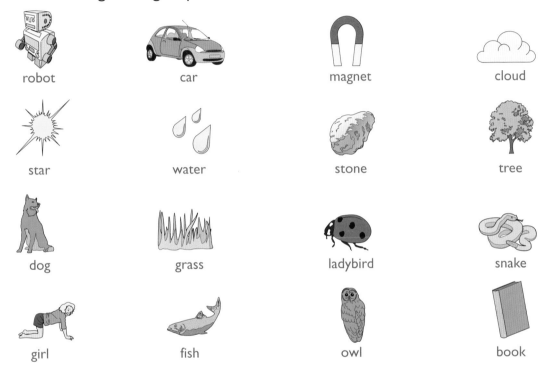

robot	car	magnet	cloud
star	water	stone	tree
dog	grass	ladybird	snake
girl	fish	owl	book

Give each group of objects a name and decide which features are common to the objects in each group. Compare your ideas with other groups in your class. Did you all come up with similar ideas?

Now make three headings in your book: 'Alive', 'Once alive' and 'Never alive'. Sort the objects into these three groups. As a class, discuss how you have grouped the objects. Do you all agree?

Look again carefully at the objects in the 'Alive' group. Think about and write down the ways in which these living things are similar to each other. Share these ideas with your class.

Do these similarities also apply to the group of objects that 'Once alive', or to the group of objects that 'Never alive'?

Life processes

There are millions of different kinds of living things on the Earth. Some are enormous, such as an elephant or a giant redwood tree, and some are very small, such as insects and microscopic water plants. However, all living things have certain **characteristics** that are essential for keeping them alive and healthy. We call these characteristics **life processes**.

All living things use the same life processes in order to keep healthy and stay alive. *MRS NERG* can help us to remember the seven life processes:

Movement
Only living things can move on their own.

Respiration
Most living things need **oxygen** from the air in order to release energy from their food. This process is called respiration and takes place in the body **cells** of living things.

Sensitivity
Living things are sensitive to their surroundings and can **react** to them.

Nutrition
Living things need food in order to build up their bodies and to give them energy. The process of obtaining food is called nutrition. Green plants are able to make their own food, whereas animals need to take in food from their surroundings.

To remember the seven life processes, think of MRS NERG

Excretion
Excretion is the removal of waste materials from plants and animals.

Reproduction
All living things need to reproduce to make more individuals of their **species** (type) otherwise they would become **extinct**.

Growth
All living things grow.

All living things carry out these seven life processes. Some of these processes are easier to observe than others. It is easy to see a bird eating a snail, but not so easy to see a tree using the light energy from the Sun to make its own food. It is easy to see a dog running but not so easy to see a sunflower turning to face the Sun.

Did you know?
Some living things can survive in a state where many of their life processes slow down or stop and they seem to be dead. One type of frog, the North American wood frog, becomes frozen solid in the winter! Its heart stops beating, it stops breathing and its brain stops working but most of these frogs thaw out again in the spring and return to normal life.

Exercise 1.1

Use the words in the box to complete the following sentences. Each word may be used once, more than once or not all.

> oxygen   energy   seven   reproduce   nutrition   alive   five
> excretion

1. There are _____ life processes.

2. All things that are _____ carry out these life processes.

3. Living things need food to give them _____ .

4. Most living things need _____ from the air.

5. _____ is how living things obtain their food.

6. Living things must _____ or they will become extinct.

Exercise 1.2

1. Name the seven life processes carried out by all living things.

2. What is the main difference between the way in which animals and plants obtain their food?

3. In what ways do you sense your surroundings?

4. What is meant by the term reproduction?

5. Why do most living things take oxygen from the air?

· ·

Key life processes in plants

Different parts of the plant are responsible for carrying out the various life processes.

The **flowers** are used for plant reproduction.

Some plants have scented or colourful flowers to attract insects which then transfer pollen from one similar flower to another. Other flowers rely on the wind to transfer pollen. Once fertilisation has taken place the flower will wither and die and seeds will start to form. Some of these seeds may then go on to become new plants.

Leaves are necessary for nutrition and for growth. Some leaves move and others are sensitive.

The green material (**chlorophyll**) in leaves and stems traps sunlight. The plant uses sunlight, water from the soil and gas from the air to make food in a process called **photosynthesis**. The leaves of many plants can change their position in order to absorb as much light as possible.

The leaves of some plants can sense something touching them and quickly roll up to appear less tasty. A Venus fly trap can sense when an insect lands on its leaf. It closes up and traps the insect (see *Junior Science Book 2* pages 21–22).

The **stem** is necessary for nutrition and reproduction.

The stem carries water, food and minerals around the plant and may also trap sunlight in the same way as the leaves. The stem also holds the leaves to the light and the flowers in a good position to be pollinated.

Roots are necessary for nutrition and growth.

The roots take in water and dissolved minerals from the soil. These are needed in the process of photosynthesis to make food for the plant so that it can grow healthily. The roots also hold the plant firmly in the soil so that it doesn't fall over or blow away.

To do: Plant parts

Draw a table with two columns in your book. In the first column list or draw the different parts of a plant and in the second column write down the function (job) of each part.

Now imagine that your plant has each one of its parts taken away in turn, for example, the roots. Discuss whether the plant would be healthy and able to survive without it.

Did you know?
The Titan Arum is a plant that comes from Sumatra. It produces one enormous leaf and the largest flower in the world. When fully grown, the flower is about three metres high and smells like rotting meat. Flies are attracted to the smell and enter the flower which is mimicking a juicy carcass where they could lay their eggs. They may be fooled several times, by a number of flowers and, as they move from flower to flower, will transfer pollen between them.

Key life processes in animals

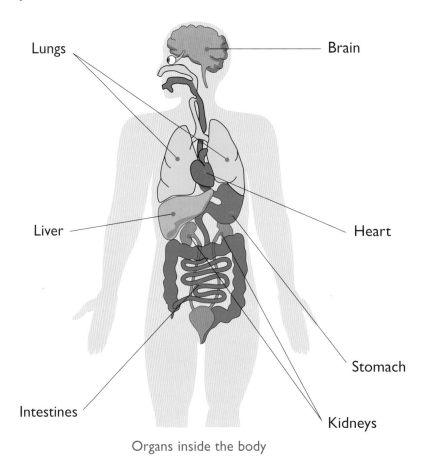

Lungs

Brain

Liver

Heart

Stomach

Intestines

Kidneys

Organs inside the body

In animals different organs of the body are responsible for carrying out the life processes. Look at the diagram above of organs in a human body.

The **brain** is necessary to control the life processes.
- The brain sends out messages to the body and controls movement and sensitivity.
- The brain helps us to think about what and when we eat.
- The brain controls our growth pattern.

The **lungs** are necessary for respiration.
- The lungs take in oxygen from the air, carry it in the blood and pass it to the body's cells.
- The lungs take **carbon dioxide** from the blood and pass it back out into the air.

The **heart** is necessary for nutrition, respiration and excretion.
● The heart pumps blood around the body.
● The blood carries oxygen from the lungs to wherever it is needed.
● The blood also takes food absorbed from the intestines and carries it around the body. The blood carries waste products to the organs responsible for excretion.

The **stomach** is necessary for nutrition.
● The stomach holds food, churning it up and mixing it with digestive juices and preparing it for the next stage of its journey into the intestines.

The **intestines** are necessary for nutrition.
● The food passes through the intestines and nutrients needed by the body are absorbed into the blood.

The **liver** is important for nutrition.
● The liver is the largest organ in the body and carries out many jobs. It helps break down the nutrients carried in the blood. It can change some poisons in the blood and make them less harmful. It stores vitamins and minerals and produces heat which warms the blood.

The **kidneys** are important for excretion.
● The kidneys are important because they clean waste products from the blood and prepare them so that the body can get rid of them.

Life story of a meerkat

The meerkat is a member of the mongoose family living in the dry harsh conditions of the Kalahari Desert in Southern Africa. They are small sociable animals living in groups of about ten, with a **dominant** male and female in the group who produce between one and three **litters** of kittens every year. The kittens are born after 60 days and feed entirely on their mother's milk for the first four weeks of life.

Meerkats are very sociable animals

As the young kittens grow they will begin to eat chewed up scraps of food brought to them by other members of the group. About nine weeks after their birth the kittens will start to explore away from the safety of the den. They follow an older meerkat who will dig for beetles, beetle larvae and geckos in the sand, allowing the younger kittens to feed and teaching them how to hunt.

While burrowing in the sand for food, the meerkats are in great danger of becoming food for other animals such as jackals and Martial eagles. Being a member of a group is a great advantage for a meerkat. While the group is feeding on the ground, one meerkat will be on guard and take on the responsibility of looking out for danger. The guard may scramble on top of a termite mound or climb in the branches of a tree in order to be in a good lookout position. The guard can then scan the sky and surroundings. If it senses danger it will give an alarm call which alerts the other members of the group who then run to the safety of a hole. The meerkats take it in turns during the day to be on guard duty, giving up the opportunity to feed while providing security for the other meerkats.

In the evening the meerkats groom each other and enjoy the last warm rays of sunshine before retreating to the safety of their underground den.

To do: Meerkat life processes

1. Think about the seven life processes you learnt about earlier in the chapter. Discuss how the meerkats carry out these life processes. Draw a picture of a group of meerkats. Use the information in the story to help you to include meerkats carrying out as many of the seven life processes as possible.

2. Make a list of some of the foods a meerkat eats during its life.

3. Animals that feed their young with milk have a special name. Find out what they are called and discover what other characteristics they have.

4. The meerkat is a very active animal, and may travel several kilometres away from the den each day in search of food. In the life story of the meerkat there are many words describing how the meerkat moves. Make a list of these words.

Exercise 1.3

Use the words in the box to complete the sentences below. Each word may be used once, twice or not at all.

| older grows milk one three beetles alarm geckos |
| run larvae younger five fly |

1. A young meerkat will feed on _____ for the first weeks of life.

2. As the meerkat _____ its diet includes other foods such as _____ , _____ and _____ .

3. Meerkats may have as many as _____ litters of kittens in a year.

4. An _____ meerkat will show a _____ meerkat how to dig and hunt for food.

5. While the group are feeding, _____ meerkat will guard the group.

6. When the guard gives an _____ call the group will _____ to safety.

Exercise 1.4: Extension questions

1. Explain why a meerkat's senses are important for the safety of the whole group.

2. In what other ways do meerkats help each other?

. . . .

Life story of an acacia tree

Acacia trees found growing in the **semi-desert** areas of Africa face many problems. However, they have developed ways of overcoming the challenges of this harsh environment. Their leaves are small, narrow and point upwards, so they absorb the light energy from the Sun but are protected from the intense heat. They also taste bitter which discourages animals from eating them. The branches not only have sharp thorns to keep herbivores away but also provide shelter for ants that sting the nose of any animal that tries to eat the leaves. The ants, however, could damage the flowers of the acacia tree, so the flowers have developed a scent that repels the ants. The wide open flowers attract other insects that help in pollination.

The acacia tree depends on elephants to help it to reproduce

After the flowers have been fertilised, the tree produces a vast quantity of seed pods. Unfortunately the seeds are attractive to beetles, which lay their eggs in the seed pods. The eggs hatch and the beetle grubs grow in the seed pod and eat the young seeds. The seed pods are also a source of food for monkeys who chew the seeds to a fine mash and destroy them. Elephants also love to eat the leaves and seed pods. They may even push a tree over in order to reach the leaves and seeds.

However, it is not all bad news for the acacia tree. Many seeds that are eaten by the elephant pass undamaged through the animal's digestive system and are passed out in the dung about 24 hours later. The seeds dispersed in this way have a good chance of survival. Any beetle grubs in them will have been killed in the elephant's gut, and they have a supply of nutritious manure to help them germinate. The seeds left on the ground under the acacia tree are unlikely ever to grow because most of them will have been destroyed by the beetle grubs or eaten by the monkeys. The tree does benefit, however, because the pods and leaves which fall from the tree, rot and return valuable nutrients to the soil.

Did you know?
Some species of bees nest in acacia trees in Africa. The buzzing sound of the bees makes elephants very nervous and they do not eat the trees where there is a bees' nest. Some farmers in areas where elephants raid crops are trying to scare the elephants away using recordings of bees buzzing.

To do: Acacia trees

Read the life story of the acacia tree carefully. See how many references you can find to life processes.

Draw a picture of an acacia tree and include the animals that are mentioned in the story.

Label your picture neatly to show where life processes are being carried out.

Exercise 1.5

Use the words in the box to complete the sentences below. Each word may be used once, twice or not at all.

elephants thorns leaves grow die light taste ants beetles heat flowers smell

1. The _____ of the acacia tree absorb the _____ energy from the Sun so that the tree can make its own food.

2. The leaves are protected by having a nasty _____ and by _____ that sting the noses of animals that try to eat the leaves.

3. The branches have sharp _____ to protect them.

4. The grubs of _____ eat the seeds in the pods.

5. Monkeys and _____ like to eat the seed pods.

6. The seeds in the dung of elephants may _____ .

Exercise 1.6

1. Explain in your own words how the acacia tree benefits from having the ants live in its branches.

2. (a) Why are the elephants so important to the seeds of the acacia tree?
   (b) Which life process do the elephants help the tree carry out?
   (c) Which life process does the tree help the elephants carry out?

3. Describe two ways in which insects help the acacia tree to carry out reproduction.

Exercise 1.7: Extension question

Choose an animal or plant you know about. Write a life story of this animal or plant, such as the ones in this chapter. Include details of how it feeds, moves, grows and reproduces. See if you can include any of the other life processes as well.

Chapter 2: Adaptation and evolution
Similarities and differences

When biologists study plants, animals and other **organisms** (living things) in a particular habitat they start by observing them carefully. They look for particular **characteristics** that will help identify an organism, and how it fits into its **community** within the habitat. When studying animals they may look at the number of legs or wings, at the colour of its body or fur, at the shape of its body or perhaps its behaviour. What characteristics do you think they might look at when studying plants?

There are millions of different types of organism alive on the Earth today. In the past there were many others which are now **extinct** such as the dinosaurs. Because there are so many organisms it would be almost impossible to study each one individually, so instead we put them into groups to study. Organisms with certain characteristics in common are put together in a particular group. You learnt about some of the animal groups in *Junior Science Book 1*.

What characteristics would help to identify this coconut crab?

Did you know?
There have been at least five periods in the Earth's history when many organisms have become extinct at the same time, usually due to changes in climate or some catastrophe. One of these was the event 65 million years ago that wiped out most of the dinosaurs. Some people think we are now in the middle of another mass extinction. Scientists have discovered that more plants and animals are becoming extinct every year, partly because of the activities of humans.

Keys

Once you have studied an organism carefully and identified its particular characteristics, it is easier to find its name and more detailed information. One way to identify an organism is to use a **key**. There are two main types of key: a **branching key** and a **number key**. If you have done a habitat study, you may have already used keys to identify the animals and plants you found.

Branching keys

A branching key is usually set out like an upside-down tree, with questions where the branches divide. The observations you make about the organism will help you to answer each question. The key shows you which path to take to the next question. Eventually you reach the stage when you can identify the organism.

Here is a simple example:

Identify the birds shown above using the branching key below:

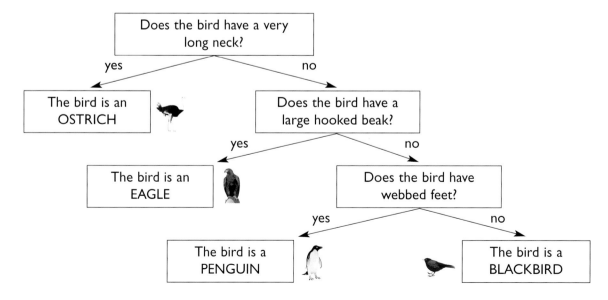

Keys can be used to identify non-living things as well as living ones. For example, you may have used the key from *Junior Science Book 1* page 55 to identify different types of rock. To use a key, you need to look carefully at the characteristics referred to in the questions. When you make a key, you need to start by looking at the organisms or objects carefully so you can use the best characteristics for identification.

To do: Make a key

1. Select four objects. Choose objects that are quite different from one another for your first key. You could choose ordinary classroom objects, such as a chair, a table, a book, etc, or some natural things, such as a shell, a pebble, a pine cone and an acorn or maybe some insects or other animals. Your teacher may give you some to choose from. If your objects are big, write the names of your objects on separate cards or pieces of paper.

2. In your group or pair, discuss what you think are the main characteristics that will help you identify these objects.

3. Start by deciding on a question you could ask that will divide the objects into two groups. The groups do not have to be equal in size. In the example above, the first question 'Does the bird have a very long neck?' resulted in a group of one (the ostrich) and a group of three (the penguin, the eagle and the blackbird). Your question must be one that has only two possible answers: yes or no.

4. On a sheet of paper, write down your first question, draw a box around it and then draw two arrows coming from the box, one with 'yes' written on it and one with 'no' written on it.

5. Take your objects or the name cards and place each of them at the end of the correct arrow.

6. If you have only one of your objects at the end of the arrow you can write 'The object is a ......' at the end of the arrow. That object has now been identified so put it or its name card somewhere out of the way. You don't need this any more.

To do: Make a key (continued)

7. Where you have more than one object at the end of the arrow, think of another question you could ask to divide these into another two groups. Write the new question at the end of the arrow and draw a neat box around it. Then draw the 'yes' and 'no' arrows below this box. Place the objects or name cards at the end of the correct arrows. Where there is only one object in the category, write 'The object is……' and put the object or card out of the way.

8. Continue this process until you have a final question which will distinguish the last two objects. You should by now have identified them all. Your key may look a bit untidy at this stage because it is sometimes hard to make everything fit. If so, it is a good idea to take a fresh piece of paper or a new page in your exercise book and make a neat copy.

9. Give one of your objects to someone in the class and see if they can use your key to identify it. If they can't, have another think about your questions. Were they clear enough? Can you think of better ones?

We can also use a branching key to identify key characteristics of a particular animal or plant we do not know. By starting at the bottom of a key and working upwards, we can unravel the key characteristics. For example, we can tell that a penguin has webbed feet, does not have a large hooked beak and does not have a long neck. What are the key characteristics of the eagle? With a very small key like this, we cannot find out very much information because there are so few questions, but a large key can tell us much more.

Number keys

Number keys are similar to branching keys in that they rely on your observing the key characteristics of the object in order to identify it. This time, instead of following a path down the page, you are told which question to go to next.

Here is a simple example:

Can you identify the leaves from the key below?

1.　The leaf is divided into several leaflets .... Go to 2
　　The leaf is a single shape .... Go to 3

2.　The leaflets are arranged like a fan .... HORSE CHESTNUT
　　The leaflets are arranged in pairs along the stalk .... ASH

3.　The leaf has prickles along its edges .... HOLLY
　　The leaf has no prickles .... Go to 4

4.　The leaf is a simple oval shape .... BEECH
　　The leaf has a wavy or lobed edge .... Go to 5

5.　The leaf has three pointed lobes .... SYCAMORE
　　The leaf has many rounded lobes .... OAK

Can you identify the key characteristics of each type of leaf from this kind of key?

Exercise 2.1

Here is a key to identify invertebrates you might find in the leaf litter of a woodland area.

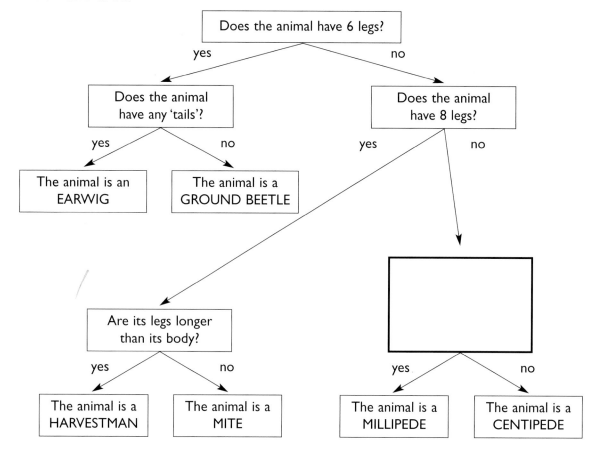

1. These pictures show four of the animals from the key. Use the key to identify them.

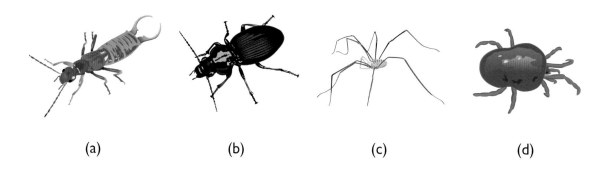

(a)   (b)   (c)   (d)

2. Here is a picture of a centipede and a millipede.

centipede    millipede

Suggest a question that might be written in the empty box in the key on page **18** to distinguish between these two animals.

3. Some children went for a walk and they saw these prints in the mud.

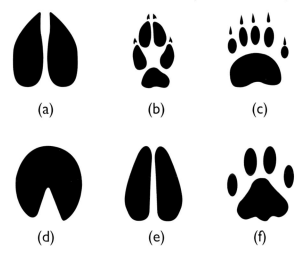

(a)	(b)	(c)
(d)	(e)	(f)

Use the key below to identify the tracks that they found.

1. Tracks made by paw prints .... Go to 2
    Tracks made by hoof prints .... Go to 4

2. The paw print has claw marks .... Go to 3
    The paw print has no claw marks .... PET CAT

3. Print from a paw with four claws .... FOX
    Print from a paw with five claws .... BADGER

4. Hoof print made by one toe .... PONY
    Hoof print made by two toes .... Go to 5

5. Tips of the hooves are pointed .... FALLOW DEER
    Tips of the hooves are rounded .... SHEEP

Exercise 2.2: Extension question

Select about six to eight members of your class. Think of the characteristics that allow you to identify them. These characteristics should be ones that you can see and that will remain the same all the time. The colour of their hair or eyes is a good starting point, but the colour of a hair band or clothing is not because these things will change from day to day.

Make a branching or number key to identify your chosen people. Be careful to ask questions that are kind and not likely to embarrass them!

You may have an opportunity to try out your key. Can someone use it to identify one of the chosen people? What happens if you try to use it to identify someone who was not in your chosen group?

Why are there so many different organisms?

We learnt earlier that there are millions of different types of organism alive on Earth today. No one really knows exactly how many but it is probably at least 10 million. Fewer than 2 million of these have been studied and given proper scientific names. There is clearly a lot of work for biologists still to do!

In any one habitat, there may be any number of different organisms, depending on the size of the habitat and the opportunities for the organisms to feed, breed and find shelter. This wide range of different living things is called **biodiversity**.

But why are there so many living things? One reason is that living things change over time. They become better **adapted** to life in a particular habitat. Each habitat has different conditions, different challenges and different opportunities and so each may have slightly different varieties of animals and plants living within it. Animals in two or more different habitats may come from the same group but have differences in their body shapes or behaviour in order to cope with the particular conditions in their habitat.

Three foxes

Red fox

You will probably recognise this animal. It is a red fox and is seen almost everywhere in Britain. It is a clever animal and able to adapt its behaviour to allow it to live successfully in a range of habitats. In towns and cities, it is commonly seen in gardens. It will eat fruit, insects and earthworms as well as catching rats, mice and birds. It will

The red fox is commonly seen in towns as well as in the country

also raid dustbins. Like all foxes it has eyes on the front of its head, to allow it to judge distances. This shows us it is a **predator**.

In the country, a red fox will catch rabbits, pheasants and small rodents, raid nests for eggs and forage in the hedgerows for fruit. It will take the opportunity to kill and eat chickens or ducks if their owners do not lock them up at night. The red fox is agile and quick, with good eyesight and hearing. Its reddish brown colour seems quite bright when it is out in the open but provides good camouflage in woodland.

Arctic fox

This is a different **species** of fox. It lives in cold areas in the far north of Europe and North America where temperatures can drop to −50 °C or lower in winter. This fox is a little smaller and stockier than the red fox and its coat is much thicker. The Arctic fox's fur consists of two different types of hair. The under fur is thick and soft. It traps air and acts as a good insulator. Over the top of this is a

The Arctic fox is well adapted to very cold conditions

layer of coarser, stronger fur that is waterproof. The Arctic fox's winter fur is the warmest fur of any animal, even warmer than that of the polar bear.

It also has fur on the underside of its feet which helps it walk on icy surfaces as well as keeping its paws warm. Extra blood vessels in the feet help to stop the fox's feet from freezing and sticking to the cold ice. It has a long, bushy tail which it uses to reduce heat loss by covering its nose and face as it curls up in a snow hollow during stormy weather. The Arctic fox has small ears and short legs, because these are areas where heat can be lost easily. It also has a thick layer of body fat.

The fur of the Arctic fox is pure white in winter when the ground is covered with snow but becomes mottled with brown when the snow melts in the short Arctic summer. This great camouflage helps it to get close to its prey without being seen.

Arctic foxes eat a lot of small rodents called lemmings. In summer, lemmings often breed very successfully and the foxes have a lot to eat. In the winter the lemmings spend most of their time in tunnels in the snow so the foxes need their very good hearing and sense of smell to find them. If the fox manages to kill more than it can eat, it will bury the extra in the snow or in the frozen ground. The food will stay quite fresh until the fox wants to eat it, just as food keeps fresh in the fridge or freezer at home. Like their red cousins, Arctic foxes are quite adaptable in their behaviour. If there are no lemmings around they will eat seal pups, scavenge on the bodies of animals that die in the harsh weather or eat the remains of a polar bear kill.

The fennec fox's large ears help it to stay cool

Fennec fox

Fennec foxes live in the deserts of northern Africa and the Middle East where it is very hot and dry. They are tiny and are the smallest members of the fox family, but they have huge ears that look as if they belong to a different animal entirely! These massive ears allow excess heat to travel out of the fox's body and into the air, keeping the fox cool.

Fennec foxes have quite thick fur. This keeps them cool in the hot daytime and warm at night when it gets cold. They have fur on their feet to stop them burning themselves on the hot sand. This fur also gives the feet a larger surface area and acts like a snowshoe, helping to stop the fox sinking into the soft sand.

Like the other foxes, fennec foxes will eat whatever they can find. This may include small rodents, lizards, insects, birds' eggs and plant material. Because there is so little water available in their habitat, they have developed the ability to survive for long periods without drinking.

All three foxes are well adapted to living in their particular habitat. Each of the habitats is very different and so, although the foxes are all from the same family and have many similarities, they also have some important differences.

Two plants
Bluebells

Here is a plant you may recognise. It is our native bluebell and is found in deciduous woodlands.

Bluebell leaves and flowers are produced from **bulbs** found underground. In the spring, as soon as the weather begins to warm up a little, the bluebell leaves begin to push up through the soil. They grow very quickly and soon the

Bluebells flower early, before the leaves of the woodland trees are fully open

blue flowers open and carpet the floor of the woodland. The attractive blue petals on the flowers indicate they are insect-pollinated, but there are not very many insects around early in the year, and a late frost can damage or kill the flowers. So, why do bluebells flower so early?

The woodland trees, forming the **canopy** above the bluebells, are deciduous and lose their leaves in the winter. When there are no leaves on the trees, light can reach the floor of the wood more easily. Plants growing there can absorb enough light to carry out photosynthesis and make a lot of food. Some of this food gives them the energy to grow and to make flowers and the rest is stored in the bulbs under the ground.

Soon after the bluebell flowers appear, the leaves begin to grow on the trees. The light levels on the floor of the wood gradually decrease which means there is less and less light energy for the plants to carry out photosynthesis. The bluebell must reproduce quickly in the short time before this happens. The flowers are sweetly scented and contain nectar to attract the few insects. After fertilisation, lots of seeds form in rounded seed cases. The leaves of the plant then begin to die and, after a very short time, you would never know that there had been any bluebells at all. All through the summer, autumn and winter, the plant is hidden underground as a bulb packed with food to help it grow new leaves the following spring.

The bluebell stores food in the bulb to help it survive

But what happens if there are no insects one year or the flowers are damaged by frost so they cannot make seeds? The bluebell plant has another trick to help it to reproduce. It can make tiny little bulbs attached to the main bulb under the ground. These gradually grow and, after a year or two, can break away from the parent bulb and become a separate plant. The bluebell is clearly well adapted to the conditions under the trees in deciduous woodland.

This cactus's stem is a water store and the leaves have become spines

Cacti

A cactus is very different to a bluebell. To start with, where are its leaves? It is fat and prickly and not at all like a typical plant.

Cacti are adapted to life in very hot, dry desert conditions. In this environment normal leaves would quickly dry and shrivel up, and then not be able to carry out photosynthesis. Cactus leaves have become hard, sharp spines, which protect the plant from hungry, thirsty animals that might want to eat it. They do not contain chlorophyll and no longer carry out photosynthesis to make food for the plant. Instead, the cactus stem has taken on the role of food production from the leaves. It has become a big water reservoir and, because it is so large, has a bigger surface area than most plant stems, which allows it to absorb enough light for photosynthesis.

The shape of the cactus is also an important **adaptation**. If there is any rain or dew, it collects on the surface of the plant. Its shape makes sure that any water runs down to the roots where it can be taken up into the water store in the stem. To make sure the valuable water is not lost through evaporation, the cactus is covered in a very thick waxy waterproof layer, which is also quite tough for animals to eat.

· ·

Exercise 2.3

Use the words in the box to complete the sentences below. Each word may be used once, more than once or not at all.

> water store   ears   dustbins   kitchens   spines   adaptations
> eaten   lemmings   chickens   prey   pheasants   fruit   predators
> leaves   light   two   rabbits   bulb   three

1. Animals and plants often have special _____ to help them to survive in their habitats.

2. Foxes have eyes on the front of their heads because they are _____ .

3. Red foxes that live in towns will often raid _____ to get food.

4. In the country, red foxes may eat _____ , _____ or _____ .

5. Arctic foxes have _____ types of hair to trap heat and keep them dry.

6. Arctic foxes eat a lot of _____ .

7. Fennec foxes have big _____ to take heat away from their bodies and keep them cool.

8. Bluebells flower early before the trees grow _____ which block out the _____ .

9. The leaves of cacti have changed to become _____ to protect the plant from being _____ .

10. The large stem of a cactus is a _____ _____ .

· ·

Exercise 2.4

1. Look back at the section on foxes (pages 21–22).

   (a) List as many similarities as you can between the three foxes' bodies and their behaviour.

   (b) List as many differences as you can identify between the Arctic fox and the red fox.

   (c) Why would the fennec fox not be able to survive in the Arctic?

2. (a) Why do bluebells flower early in the spring?

   (b) What problems might there be when flowering early in the year?

   (c) How do the bluebell plants survive during summer, autumn and winter when they have no leaves to make food?

3. Describe in your own words how a cactus is adapted to survive in the desert.

To do: Spot the adaptations

Read the following description of a camel.

The best-known desert animal is probably the camel. It is extremely well adapted to desert life, which is why the people living there rely on it for transport across the desert sands. The type of camel most often found in the Sahara is the one-humped dromedary camel. The camel's hump is an important adaptation. It is not used to store water as many people believe.

Instead it is full of fat, which provides the camel with a food store, helping it to survive many days travelling between oases. When a camel comes to a pool of water, it can drink up to 100 litres in one go and then store it in its large stomach.

To save water and prevent themselves from becoming **dehydrated**, camels do not sweat unless their bodies warm up to over 40 °C. Most animals would die if they got this hot. Camels also lose less water through their nostrils than other animals. Their long legs keep their bodies further from the hot sand and their thick fur reflects heat away from the body to keep them cool.

Camels are able to close their nostrils and have very long eyelashes and hairs inside their ears. These adaptations are very useful in sandstorms because they stop the sand blowing into their noses, eyes and ears. Their large flat feet are ideal for walking across soft sand.

1. You need a picture of a camel in the centre of a sheet of paper. Your teacher may give you one of these or you could draw it yourself. Label the diagram neatly, clearly showing the ways in which the camel is adapted to life in the desert.

2. Make up at least five questions about the camel. Make sure that the answers to these questions can be found in the passage. Write each question in your book and then write a model answer to it, including as much detail as possible. See if your partner can answer the questions.

3. Think of one or two questions about camels that cannot be answered by reading the passage. Write them down and try to find the answers from books or the internet.

Camouflage

One of the most obvious ways in which an animal is adapted to its habitat is its colouring, otherwise known as its **camouflage**. Camouflage helps animals to hide. Prey animals need to hide from predators. Predators need to hide so that their prey does not see them lying in wait or approaching. Even some plants are camouflaged. For instance, the stone plant, found in stony deserts, looks exactly like the stones that surround it. It is very hard to spot.

Stone plants are hard to see amongst pebbles

Can you spot the nightjar?

Some animals are so well camouflaged that it is hard to see them even when you know they are there. This bird, a nightjar, which keeps its eyes almost shut, looks just like some fallen leaves or a dead twig and could easily be overlooked.

The animals in the following pictures are also well camouflaged. They are both insects. You may be able to spot them and guess what they are pretending to be!

These insects are very well camouflaged
(photograph of D. gigantea [left] courtesy of jonathansjungleroadshow.co.uk)

To do: Design an adapted creature

Can you name the seven life processes all living things carry out in order to survive? (Clue: remember MRS NERG from Chapter 1.)

An animal in its habitat needs to be able to carry out all of these life processes and may need special adaptations in order to do so successfully.

1. Imagine you are visiting a new habitat that no one else has seen before. Decide on the conditions of your new habitat. Is it hot or cold? Is there plenty of water or is it very dry? What plant life is there?

2. There are very likely to be some organisms in your new habitat that are new to science. Your job is to design a completely new creature to live in your habitat. Try to make it unlike any creature that you already know. Use your imagination to make something really different. Think about how your creature will carry out the seven life processes in its habitat. Is your creature a predator or a prey animal? If it is prey, what does it eat and what might hunt it? If it is a predator, what might it hunt? Does it need to be camouflaged?

3. Carefully draw and label a picture of your creature. Remember to show clearly how it carries out the life processes and what adaptations it has to help it survive in its habitat.

4. If you have time you could design a plant that is adapted to your habitat as well.

Evolution

We can read the story of the creation of the Heavens and Earth by God in the Bible's Book of Genesis. The holy texts of many other religions have very similar stories in them. For thousands of years these stories were all people had to help them make sense of the huge diversity of life on Earth. In *Junior Science Book 2* we learnt about how modern science has changed the way people think about Earth's place in the Universe. In the same way, people's view of the Earth's biodiversity has also changed as our understanding has grown.

In the 18th and 19th centuries people discovered strange animal and plant shapes embedded in rocks. They did not know what they were or how they came to be there. Some people said that they were nothing but patterns in the rocks that just happened to look like animals. Others thought that they were the remains of the animals and plants that were killed in the great flood that is described in the Bible and other religious texts. Nowadays we call them fossils and know that they were formed when animals and plants died and were covered by layers and layers of sediment (see *Junior Science Book 1* pages 56–58).

A fossil ammonite

As more and more fossils were found, scientists began to study them in more detail. They could see that although some of the shapes looked quite unlike anything alive on Earth, others were similar to plants and animals they could see around them. At about the same time, geologists began to realise that the Earth is millions of years old rather than a few thousand years old as people had thought. As geologists studied the fossils in the rocks, they could see that some types of animal seemed to change gradually over long periods of time. This slow change came to be known as **evolution**, though at first no one was sure how these changes happened.

In 1831, a survey ship called HMS Beagle set out on a journey around the world. It was to visit a number of places, including South America, mainly to make more accurate maps for ships.

Charles Darwin

The captain of the ship, Captain Fitzroy, invited a young man to act as his assistant and provide company on the long voyage. This man's name was Charles Darwin. He spent the journey studying the geology, plants, animals and people in the places they visited. He collected lots of specimens, many of which are now in the Natural

Darwin travelled around the world on *HMS Beagle*

History Museum in London, and wrote lots of notes about his observations. One of the places they visited was a group of islands called the Galapagos. The Galapagos Islands are west of Ecuador and on the equator. Charles Darwin observed that although the animals found on all the islands were similar, each island had slightly different versions. For example, small birds called finches were found on all the islands but had different shaped beaks on different islands. He also noticed that the giant tortoises had different shaped shells. He could see that this was because the food available on each island was slightly different but at first he could not work out how the differences had occurred.

This giant tortoise can eat plants on the ground but its low shell would make it hard to reach leaves higher up in a bush

Darwin returned home and spent many years thinking about this. Eventually, in 1859, he published his ideas in a famous book called *The Origin of Species*. In this book he suggested that because animals are born with natural differences from their parents, it is likely that these differences would make some of the offspring better adapted to their environment than others. For example, a tortoise on an island where there was no grass and where the only food was leaves on bushes, would find it easier to reach the leaves if the front of its shell was slightly more curved so that it could stretch its head up. A finch on an island where the only seeds available had very hard shells would find it easier to crack them if its beak was a bit bigger and stronger. In other places a difference might make the animal better camouflaged or better able to escape from predators. Darwin thought these creatures would be more likely to survive and reproduce and so their characteristics would become more common in the next generation. Gradually, over many generations, tortoises with very curvy shells or finches with big strong beaks would become more and more common on that particular island. Eventually, completely new species could develop in this way. Darwin called this process **natural selection**. This led to the huge variety of animals and plants that have lived since life on Earth began. Even human beings could have developed gradually from a monkey-like ancestor.

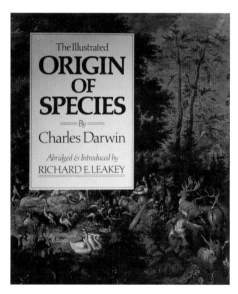

Since its publication, there have been many versions of *The Origin of Species*

Darwin's book was a best-seller but his ideas were not very popular at first. There were several reasons for this. Some people were upset because the ideas made people question the creation story in the Bible. Others were not at all happy to be told that they were descended from monkeys! Before long, however, his theory became widely accepted and it now forms the basis of our current understanding. Darwin himself was aware that his book did not explain everything, and he spent the rest of his life carrying out experiments to gather further evidence. The recent discovery of more fossil evidence is helping to fill in some of the gaps. Twentieth and twenty-first century science has also provided more evidence through the study of **genes** and how characteristics are passed from one generation to another. We now have plenty of evidence that Darwin's ideas were right but we also know that the story is a lot more complicated than he thought. There is still a lot of work to do before we understand it properly.

Did you know?
Although Charles Darwin was almost certainly the first to work out the theory of evolution by natural selection, another younger scientist called Alfred Russel Wallace also thought of the same idea at around the same

time. His essay on the subject and Darwin's book were presented to the Royal Society in London at the same time. Darwin's work is best known because he was the first to publish a book on it and he was already well-known in scientific circles. Wallace was a great admirer of Darwin and felt honoured that his work was considered alongside that of his hero.

Exercise 2.5

1. When people first saw fossils, what ideas did they have to explain them?

2. What is meant by the term 'evolution'?

3. (a) What was the name of the ship in which Charles Darwin sailed around the world?

   (b) Who was the captain of this ship?

   (c) What was Darwin's job on this voyage?

4. What is the name of the group of islands where Darwin observed giant tortoises and finches?

5. What did Darwin notice about the animals on the different islands?

6. (a) Describe in your own words the theory that Darwin suggested to explain how differences can occur in animals and plants.

   (b) What name did he give to this process?

7. Why were some people not happy about Darwin's theory?

8. Give two examples of ways in which scientists are still finding out more about how evolution occurs.

Exercise 2.6: Extension question

Use books or the internet to help you to make a map showing the route taken by the *Beagle*. See if you can find out about some of the places he visited during the four years and nine months of the trip.

Chapter 3: Life cycles

Round and round

In Chapter 1 of this book you learnt about the seven life processes that are carried out by living things. Can you remember them all?

One of these life processes is **reproduction**. No living thing can live forever, although some can live for a very long time. It is therefore essential that all living things reproduce so that the species will continue living and not become extinct.

There are lots of different ways of reproducing. Some very small organisms are just one **cell** and reproduce by splitting themselves into two.

Most larger plants and animals reproduce by joining together two cells from different individuals. One of these special cells is usually called an **egg** or **ovum** and generally comes from the female parent.

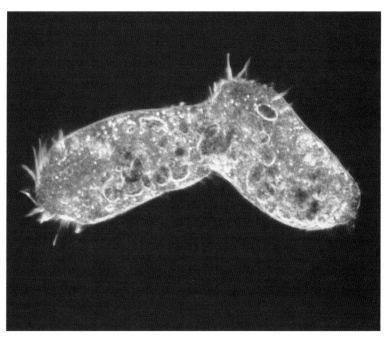

Single-celled organisms reproduce by splitting themselves into two

The male cell may be in a pollen grain or may be a **sperm** cell. These special reproduction cells are known as **gametes**. Each one contains half the information needed to make a new individual. The joining together of these two gametes is known as **fertilisation** and the resulting cell, or **zygote**, contains the whole set of information to make the new individual. This individual may grow to become an adult and then reproduce to create the next generation, and so on. This is what we call a life cycle. In *Junior Science Book 2* we learnt about how this process occurs in flowering plants. In this chapter you will learn about the life cycles of some animals.

Exercise 3.1

Use the words from the box to complete the following sentences. Each word may be used once, more than once or not at all.

> gametes   sperm   egg   one   cell   reproduce   fertilisation
> ovum   zygote   extinct   two   splitting   eat   three

1. All living things need to _____ so that their species do not become _____ .

2. Very small organisms that are made of just one _____ may reproduce by _____ the cell in two.

3. Most larger animals and plants need _____ special cells to reproduce.

4. The special cell that comes from the male parent is called a _____ .

5. The special cell that comes from the female parent is called an _____ or _____ .

6. The name given to special cells used for reproduction is _____ .

7. The joining together of two _____ is called _____ and the new cell formed when they join is called a _____ .

· ·

All change

Some of the most interesting life cycles are those in which the animal changes its form completely when it becomes an adult. Can you think of any examples of this?

Moths and butterflies spend their early lives as caterpillars before changing into a beautiful winged adult form. Many other insects, such as flies and beetles, spend their early lives as grubs with no legs or wings. This huge change of form is called **metamorphosis**. Let's look at the life cycle of one of these animals in more detail.

The Red Admiral butterfly is often seen in our gardens during the summer, feeding on nectar from flowers. Most Red Admirals migrate to the UK from warmer places in Europe, arriving in May or June, although some will have spent the winter in barns or sheds, sheltering from the cold. The adult females lay their eggs on the leaves of nettle plants, and the young caterpillars hatch out after a week or so, depending on the weather. The caterpillars spend about three to four weeks feeding on the nettle leaves. When they are not feeding, they hide in little tents made by pulling the edges of a leaf together. As they grow bigger they make themselves bigger tents.

When they have grown big enough, they will pull several leaves together using silk they have spun, hide inside the tent they have made and fix themselves firmly to a leaf. Their skin hardens and

turns a greyish brown colour. They stay like this for about two or three weeks. This stage of the insect's development is called a **pupa**. Inside the hard skin the animal gradually changes so that the body is no longer caterpillar shaped but has the three-part body of an insect. Three pairs of long, jointed legs appear on the thorax (the middle section of a three-part body). Two pairs of wings are formed, all crumpled up to fit inside the

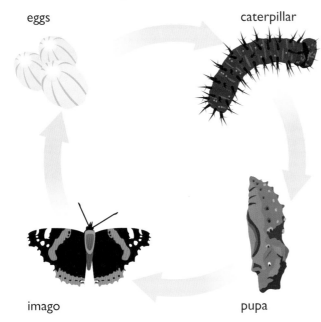

eggs

caterpillar

imago

pupa

The life cycle of a butterfly

pupa's skin. When all the changes have taken place, the skin splits open and the adult, or **imago**, pulls itself out. It pumps blood into the wings to stretch them out and spends some time sitting in the sun so that they dry and harden. The butterfly will then suddenly take wing to start a new life as a flying insect, feeding on nectar and finding a mate. Another set of eggs will then be laid and the life cycle begins again.

Did you know?
Some species of moth, for example the spindle ermine moth, lay hundreds of eggs on one plant. When the caterpillars hatch out they spin a huge tent of silk over and around the bush they are on. They can then feed in safety, protected from predators.

One group of vertebrates also undergo metamorphosis in their life cycle. These are **amphibians**, most of which lay their eggs in water and have young that are very different to the adult. The common frog, found in pools all over the country, is a good example of this.

Adult frogs are well adapted to life in water. They have webbed feet for swimming and eyes on the top of their heads so they can look out for prey or predators above the water, while keeping their bodies under the water. Their skin is specially adapted to allow them to absorb oxygen from the water so that they can spend long periods under water without breathing. In spite of all these adaptations, adult frogs spend more time on land than in the water, living in damp places so that their delicate skin does not dry out, and feeding by catching flies with their long sticky tongues.

In spring, frogs make their way to water, usually to the same pool where they began life. The males usually arrive first and begin croaking noisily to attract the females. When a female arrives the males compete to reach her. Sometimes a female may be mobbed by as many as ten males.

Frogs need to return to water to breed; their eggs are called spawn

She will lay her eggs in the water and the winning male will release a cloud of sperm at the same time. Most of the eggs will be fertilised and grow a protective layer of jelly around them. They can be found in huge clumps in some ponds. The jelly prevents the developing embryos from drying out and makes it a little less easy for predators to eat them.

After about a week a tiny comma-shaped **tadpole** forms and the jelly dissolves, releasing the tadpole into the water. At first the tadpole feeds on tiny water plants called **algae**, scraping them off the surface of plants with a rasping mouth which is on the underside of its head. These tiny tadpoles have feathery **gills** on the outside of their body but after a week or two these are replaced by internal gills. At around this time the

After a few weeks the tadpoles begin to grow legs

tadpole's diet also changes and it begins to feed on tiny water fleas and other invertebrates.

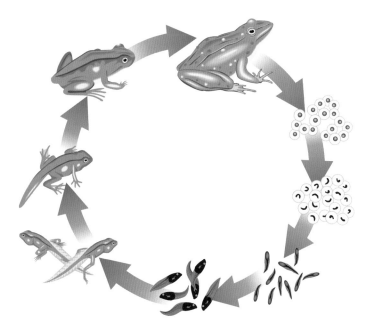

The life cycle of a frog

About seven weeks after hatching, the back limbs begin to grow. These are tiny and useless at first, but they gradually grow bigger and stronger. Soon the front legs also begin to grow, the eyes become bigger and the tail starts to shrink and the young frog develops lungs to breathe in air. Eventually, at the age of about 12–14 weeks, a tiny frog emerges from the water for the first time.

Did you know?
The axolotl is a type of amphibian found in Mexico. It starts its life cycle like other amphibians by laying eggs which hatch into tadpoles. The tadpoles of the axolotl grow front and back legs but they never complete metamorphosis, and remain in the water breathing through the gills they keep. There may be fewer than 1000 of these curious animals left in the wild although, as they are popular pets, many exist in captivity.

Exercise 3.2

Use the words from the box to complete the following sentences. Each word may be used once, more than once or not at all.

> cabbage   metamorphosis   tents   imago   pupa   nettle   sheds

1.   Some animals undergo a huge change in form, called _____ during their life cycles.

2.   Red Admiral butterflies lay eggs on _____ plants.

3.   The caterpillars protect themselves by making _____ out of leaves.

4.   When the caterpillar is big enough it will fix itself to a leaf and turn into a _____ .

5.   Inside the _____ the caterpillar changes form to become an adult butterfly, called an _____ .

Exercise 3.3

1.   Explain what is meant by the word 'metamorphosis'.

2.   Name two animals that undergo metamorphosis in their life cycle.

3.   What is the food plant for Red Admiral caterpillars?

4.   How would you recognise a Red Admiral pupa?

5.   Describe the changes that occur to the caterpillar while it is in the pupa.

6. What happens when all these changes have taken place?

7. To which group of vertebrates does the frog belong?

8. Where do frogs lay their eggs?

9. What name is given to frogs' eggs?

10. What differences are there between a tadpole and an adult frog?

Exercise 3.4: Extension questions

1. A pond will often contain frog spawn from many different frogs.

   (a) Suggest one reason why it might be good for the baby frogs if thousands of eggs are laid in the same pond.

   (b) Suggest a reason why the presence of so many tadpoles in the same pond might be a disadvantage.

2. In the rainforest, tree frogs spend their lives in the branches of trees and seldom come to the ground. Where do you think they might lay their eggs? (You could do some research to find out if you do not know the answer.)

Our own life cycle

Human babies look like a smaller version of their parents

Have you ever seen a lamb being born or a chick hatching from an egg? Maybe your dog has had puppies. You may have watched a film of baby animals being born. Many baby animals look similar to their parents. They may be blind and hairless or have fluff instead of feathers but, in general, they are the same shape, just rather smaller. They will grow without any major change, or metamorphosis, into adults.

When a human baby is born, people often look to see if it looks most like its mother or its father. In fact, a baby will be like its mother in some ways and like its father in other ways. To understand why, we need to think about how babies are formed and what happens as a baby grows up.

A new-born baby is pretty helpless. It doesn't seem to do much other than eat and sleep, but it is doing a lot of learning. It needs to learn how to feed, how to recognise its parents and how to tell them when it is hungry, tired or uncomfortable. It looks around all the time as its brain begins to make sense of the images it sees and the sounds it hears. It is also growing fast. At first, its food is only milk, but after a while it will begin to eat solid foods too. It will learn to smile, try to communicate and begin to move around, to play, to feed itself and to walk. All this time it needs adult care.

As a toddler it may begin to go to places away from home where it can learn to play with other children and, after a few years, it will probably go to school. All this time it is growing and learning to do new things.

Puberty

As girls and boys grow up, they begin to notice changes happening in their bodies. These changes begin at different ages in different people but sooner or later they happen to everyone. The stage in our lives when these changes take place is called **puberty**. Puberty is the time when our bodies begin to get ready for adult life.

Some of the changes are particular to girls and some to boys. Boys become stronger and their voices 'break' (become deeper). They begin to grow hair on their faces and the **penis** becomes larger.

Girls may notice that their **breasts** begin to get larger. Breasts are important because they are the place where milk is made for human babies. Young girls do not need large breasts but the breasts begin to grow at puberty so that when the girl is old enough to have children of her own she will be able to provide the nutritious milk that a baby needs for healthy growth. Other changes also happen inside girls' bodies at this time.

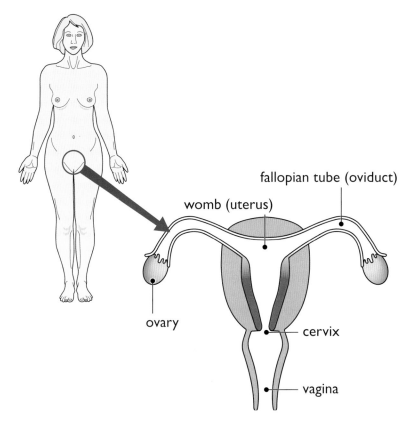

Inside a woman's body there are two **ovaries** where eggs are made. These are joined to a place called the **womb** or **uterus** by two tubes, called **fallopian tubes** or **oviducts**. The womb is the place where a baby grows until it is big enough to be born. When a girl goes through puberty, the womb begins to develop a thick lining, full of blood vessels. If a baby were inside the womb, these would provide the oxygen and nutrients it would need.

Each month one of the ovaries releases an egg into the tube connecting it to the womb. It is really important that the womb is perfect for a baby to grow in, so it renews itself monthly. If the egg is not able to develop into a baby, it passes out through the opening called the **vagina**. The thick lining of the womb begins to break away. The blood that was in the lining passes out of the body through the vagina. This monthly bleeding is called a **period** and usually lasts for a few days. During this time a girl will need to use **sanitary towels** or **tampons** to absorb the blood. The lining of the womb is then replaced with a new one ready for the next egg. This monthly cycle of changes to the womb is known as the **menstrual cycle**.

Some changes happen to both boys and girls. Some people find the skin on their faces becomes greasier and they may get spots. Most people find that the smell of their bodies changes, especially when they get a bit hot and sweaty. Hair grows thicker in certain places on their bodies. Many young people become rather moody during puberty and they begin to care a lot more about what other people think of them. It can be a very bewildering time and it is important to understand what is happening so that everyone can be supportive of each other.

Exercise 3.5

1. Describe some of the things that a human baby needs to learn in the first few months of its life.

2. What name is given to the part of a human's life when they change from being a child to being an adult?

3. Describe some of the changes that happen to boys' bodies during the time you have named in question 2.

4. Girls find that their breasts grow bigger when they grow up. What is the function of a woman's breasts?

5. What is happening when a girl has a period?

6. Describe some other changes that may be experienced by both boys and girls as they go through this time of change.

Making a baby

As with most animals and plants, making a human baby takes two parents: a mother and a father. A baby can only start to grow if one of the eggs from the mother's ovaries is fertilised by a sperm cell from the father. The egg and the sperm cell (the gametes) each contain half a set of information for making a new person. When they join together a full set of information is created, half of which comes from the baby's mother and half from the father. This is why each baby is a bit like both its parents.

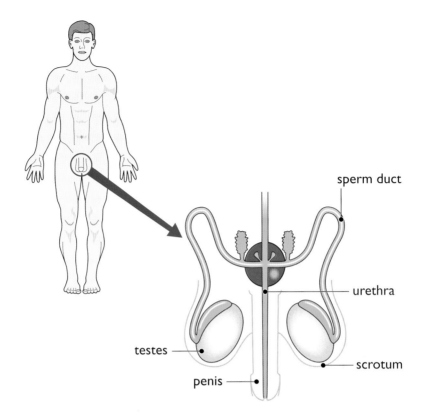

Sperm cells are made in two special places, called **testes**. These hang outside a man's body in sacks of skin called the **scrotum**. When a man and a woman have decided that they want to have a baby, they get very close together and the man pushes his penis into the woman's vagina. The sperm cells rush out of the testes and up the tube through the middle of the penis, called the **urethra**, and out into the woman's vagina.

Sperm cells have tiny tails and are able to swim. They swim up through the womb in search of the egg. When a sperm finds the egg in the fallopian tube, it burrows in and joins with the egg to fertilise it. The two special cells, or gametes, have now become one zygote. This will begin to divide into two, then four, then eight and so on. Eventually a little ball of cells will reach the womb and bury itself in the thick lining. This little ball of cells develops over nine months into a baby.

The growing baby

When a baby is developing in the womb, it is known as a **fetus**. As the fetus begins to develop, it needs plenty of oxygen and nutrients. It cannot breathe

and eat for itself so the mother has to do these things for it. A structure called the **placenta** is created to join the growing fetus to the thick lining of the womb. The fetus is attached to the placenta by the **umbilical cord**. The baby's blood flows through the cord into the placenta and back to the baby's body. The placenta is joined to the lining of the womb, where there are lots of little blood vessels containing the mother's blood. Oxygen and nutrients from the mother's blood can pass into the baby's blood and be transported to the baby. Carbon dioxide and other waste materials from the fetus are passed into the mother's blood so that the mother's body can get rid of them. The mother's blood and the baby's blood do not mix; materials are passed through the walls of the blood vessels from one to the other.

To protect the fetus from injury while it is in the womb, it is surrounded by a bag of watery fluid called the **amniotic sac**. The growing fetus floats in this liquid. It also swallows it and takes it in and out of its lungs, helping to develop the muscles it will need to eat and breathe when it is born. This liquid also helps to keep the fetus at a constant temperature.

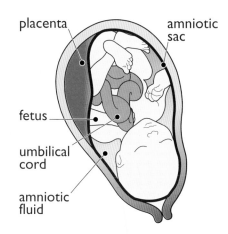

The baby in the womb is provided with oxygen and nutrients through the placenta and umbilical cord

Birth

A human baby takes nine months to develop in the womb before it is ready to be born. When the time is near, most babies will turn upside down so that their heads are born first. The mother will begin to feel the muscles around the womb contract and relax as they begin to push the baby out of the womb. The narrow passage through the **cervix** and vagina (see the diagram on page 42) will have become quite stretchy so there is room for the baby to be squeezed out into the world. When the baby is born, a nurse or doctor will cut the umbilical cord. This does not hurt the baby because there are no **nerves** in the cord. The remains of the cord will shrivel up and this becomes the baby's belly button. A little time after the baby is born, the placenta is also passed out of the mother's body. The baby will be encouraged to take its first breaths and soon will be happily feeding on milk from its mother's breasts. A new person has been born.

Like all baby mammals a human baby is fed on milk from its mother's breasts

Exercise 3.6

1. (a) What name is given to the structures in a woman's body that produce eggs?

    (b) How often is an egg normally released from these structures?

    (c) What is the name of the tubes that link this structure to the womb (uterus)?

2. How does the womb (uterus) prepare each month to support a baby?

3. (a) Describe what happens each month if the egg is not able to become a baby.

    (b) What name is given to this process?

4. Where in a man's body are sperm produced?

5. Describe briefly how sperm get into the woman's body.

6. Where in the woman's body does fertilisation take place?

7. What name is given to the baby when it is developing in the womb?

8. Describe how the growing baby is provided with nutrients and oxygen. Use the terms 'placenta' and 'umbilical cord' in your answer.

9. How is the developing baby protected from injury?

10. How long does it take for a human baby to develop in the womb?

Chapter 4: Healthy living

A healthy, balanced diet

Living things need energy to carry out life processes and energy comes from food. Plants make their own food using light energy from the Sun, gases in the air, and water and minerals from the soil. Animals, however, have to catch or find their food in order to get their energy.

Humans used to obtain their food by hunting for meat and fish and gathering fruit and berries. After a time, they began to grow crops and harvest them, developing tools to help them. They tamed animals and reared them to supply their families with the meat and milk they needed. Nowadays, in many parts of the world, food is much easier to find. There are often shops and markets offering a wide variety of foods. Food is transported all around the world so the selection of food available in many

Foods, such as fish, can be preserved by smoking

shops is enormous. We can also **preserve** food to make it last longer. People used to salt meat and smoke fish to stop it rotting. Now we can put it in cans, dry it and freeze it, so making it available all the year round, and not just in the season when it is harvested.

It is important we choose foods that will provide us with the energy we need to keep us healthy. With so much food available it is important that we understand which foods are good for us and which are not.

In *Junior Science Book 1* we learnt that food contains special substances called **nutrients** and that different foods contain different nutrients. It is important that our **diet** (the range of food and drink we take into our bodies) includes all the nutrients our bodies need to stay healthy.

A healthy, balanced diet should include nutrients for energy: **carbohydrates** and **fats**.

- There are two types of carbohydrates: **starch** and **sugars**. Starchy carbohydrates found in bread, pasta, rice and cereals, give us slow-release energy that lasts us through the day. Sugary carbohydrates, found in cakes, biscuits and fruit, release energy quickly. Too much sugar can cause tooth decay, so we should try not to eat too many sugary foods.

- Fats are important in our diet. They are found in meat, fish and dairy products and also in foods such as crisps and chips. We store fat under the skin which helps to keep us warm and provides a useful source of energy. Too much fat can make us overweight and cause heart disease and diabetes.

A healthy, balanced diet should include nutrients for growth and repair: **proteins**. Proteins are found in meat, fish, eggs and dairy products, and also in nuts, beans and lentils.

We can get iron from red meats

A healthy, balanced diet should also include nutrients for maintaining good health: **vitamins** and **minerals**. These are found in a wide variety of foods, particularly dairy products, fruit and vegetables. In *Junior Science Book 1* we learnt about a disease called scurvy, caused by a diet lacking in vitamin C. Minerals are important to keep our bodies functioning properly. For example, we need **iron** from red meats and green vegetables to make red blood cells (see page 54). If we do not have enough iron in our diets we may become **anaemic**. We would feel very tired because the blood would not have enough red blood cells to carry all the oxygen we need around our body. **Calcium**, from milk and other dairy products, is needed to help our bones to grow properly and remain strong.

Calcium from dairy products is important for strong bones

The food pyramid that we learnt about in *Junior Science Book 1* helps us to remember that we need to eat more of the foods at the bottom of the pyramid: the carbohydrates (pasta, bread and rice), and less of the foods at the top: the fats and sugars (cakes, sweets and fizzy drinks).

A healthy balanced diet also includes plenty of **fibre**. This is the indigestible parts of the food: the skins and peel and outer casing of seeds and nuts. These, along with plenty of fluids, help the intestines move the food along the digestive system.

Choosing what we eat

We should eat a wide variety of different foods to have a healthy, balanced diet. However, some people, either by choice or for health reasons, avoid eating certain foods and a number of religions do not allow people to eat certain foods. **Vegetarians** prefer not to eat meat. Some people, for example those suffering from the disease called **diabetes**, should not eat too much sugar. People who are allergic to certain foods, for example nuts or dairy products must avoid these. For these reasons it is important we know the ingredients in the foods we eat. If you look on the label or packaging material of foods you will see a box labelled **Ingredients** and a chart labelled **Nutrition information**.

Ingredients are the different food items which have been used in the recipe, with the largest quantity ingredient listed first and the smallest last.

Food labels help us to select healthy foods

The nutritional information lists the nutrients that will be found in the food: carbohydrates (starch and sugars), proteins, fats, vitamins and minerals. Often the quantity of salt (sodium) used in the recipe will also be listed. There are usually two columns: one shows the amount of nutrients contained in one serving and the other the amount of nutrients found in 100 g of the product.

There is also a list of any **additives**, such as **colourings** and **preservatives** that may have been used. Some people are allergic to these and so it is important to indicate if the food item contains any additives. Many labels have a 'traffic light' indicator to show whether the food is healthy or not. A food with a lot of fat or sugar in it, for example, would be marked with a red traffic light and one with very low fat or sugar, or maybe containing a lot of healthy nutrients, such as vitamins or fibre, would be marked with a green light.

To do: Food labels

1. Make a collection of food labels and sort them into groups. You could make a group of foods that contain nuts, a group of foods that are suitable for vegetarians, a group with no added sugar or a group with no artificial colours. There will be many ways to group your labels. Compare your findings with the rest of the class.

2. Choose labels from two similar products, for example cereals, one of which is plain and the other of which has a sugar or chocolate coating. Compare the levels of sugar and fats in the two products. When you are making a comparison be sure to look at the portion size at the top of the column. Discuss in your class why you think the label has two columns, one for the nutrients in a portion, and the other for the nutrients in 100 g.

Exercise 4.1

Use the words in the box to fill in the gaps in the sentences below. Each word may be used once, more than once or not at all.

pyramid   food   proteins   nutrients   balanced   minerals
carbohydrates   vitamins   fats   sugars   anaemic

1. Food contains special substances called _____ .

2. The nutrients for energy are _____ and _____ .

3. _____ are important for growth and repair.

4. The nutrients for maintaining good health are _____ and _____ .

5. It is important that we have a healthy, _____ diet.

6. The food _____ will help us remember which foods we should eat more of.

Exercise 4.2

1. Explain in your own words why it is important to have a label with nutrition information on food packaging.

2. Why do some food labels have 'traffic light' colours on the nutrition label?

3. Explain why labels have two columns, one giving the information for a portion size and the other giving the information for 100 g.

Exercise 4.3: Extension questions

1. Suggest why it is important that a bag of oven chips should have a nutrition label on the packaging whereas loose potatoes have no label.

2. In the shop you can choose between fresh carrots, canned carrots or frozen carrots. Explain the reasons why you might choose to buy each of these.

Testing foods

To create an accurate food label, food scientists find out about the different nutrients contained in each food. They use a number of different tests to find out which nutrients are in the food and how much there is in one helping or in 100 g. Most of these tests are now done by machine but some tests are quick and easy and we can try two of them in the classroom.

To do: Test foods for starch and fat

You can find out if a food contains starch by using a liquid called **iodine solution**. Iodine solution is an orange-brown colour but when it comes into contact with starch it turns blue-black.

There are several ways of detecting fat in foods. The method you will use is a simple one that does not need any chemicals. Foods containing fat leave a greasy mark when pressed onto a piece of paper so we can use this to detect the presence of fat.

You will need:

- small samples of different foods
- container to put each food in while it is being tested for starch
- pipette
- iodine solution
- safety goggles or glasses
- piece of white paper marked into sections, one for each food

Safety first

Iodine solution can harm your eyes so wear safety glasses or goggles when doing this experiment.

Do not put any of the foods into your mouth.

Warning! Iodine solution can stain your hands and clothes.

1. Prepare a table like this in your book or on a worksheet.

Food being tested	Colour of iodine on the food	Does the food contain starch?	Does it leave a greasy mark on the paper?	Does the food contain fat?

2. Take a small piece of the food to be tested and place it in the container you have been given.

3. Use a pipette to drip two or three drops of iodine solution onto the food.

4. Look carefully to observe any colour change. Record your results carefully in the table.

5. Next take another small piece of the food and place it in one of the sections on your piece of white paper.

6. Use a pencil to write the name of the food in the section. Press the food sample firmly onto the paper and then tip it off again.

7. Leave the paper in a warm place for a while before checking for a greasy mark and recording your results in the table. Many foods contain a lot of water and will leave a wet mark on the paper. This wet mark will dry after a time but a greasy mark will not. You need to let the paper dry before you can tell which foods have left a greasy mark and which have left a wet mark.

When you have tested all the foods, remember to wash your hands.

Look carefully at your results. Which foods contain starch? Which ones contain fat? Do any of them contain both starch and fat? Discuss with your partner or group where each of these foods would appear in a food pyramid. Which of the foods do you think you should eat most of and which should you avoid eating too often?

Digestion

The food we eat contains important nutrients but they are not in a form which can be used by our organs. The food needs to be broken down so it is small enough to be passed around the body. This process is called **digestion**.

The first stage of digestion takes place in our mouth. We chew food to make it soft and it is mixed with a liquid called **saliva**. Saliva contains a special chemical called an **enzyme** which begins the digestion process. The food is then swallowed and passes into the stomach where more enzymes and acid continue the digestion process.

In the final stage of digestion, the food passes into the **small intestine**. The digested nutrients are able to move through the walls of the intestine and into the blood so that they can be transported around the body.

Keeping the machine running smoothly

We learnt in *Junior Science Book 1* that the human body is the cleverest and most complicated machine ever built. All the **organs** work together controlled by the **brain**. In this chapter we have learnt that the fuel needed to keep our bodies running smoothly is provided by the food we eat. The human body machine also needs a transport system to connect all the organs together, keep them supplied with everything they need and remove all waste products.

The **blood** circulatory system provides this vital transport. Our blood contains **red blood cells**, which are responsible for transporting oxygen around the body. It also contains **white blood cells** which fight disease, and special chemicals. All of these are carried in a clear liquid called **plasma**. Nutrients also dissolve in the plasma and are transported around the body. The pump that keeps our blood moving is the **heart**, a powerful organ about the size of a clenched fist. It pumps about 5 litres of blood every minute, sending it on its journey around the body.

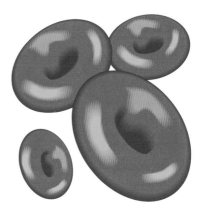

Red blood cells transport oxygen around the body

The blood is pumped by the heart through a system of blood vessels: **arteries**, **capillaries** and **veins**. The arteries are strong wide tubes and carry the blood away from the heart. The arteries divide into narrower tubes and eventually into a fine mesh of smaller tubes called capillaries. The oxygen, water and digested food nutrients that are carried in the blood are able to pass through the thin walls of the capillaries and into the cells throughout the body. Carbon dioxide and waste products from the cells are then passed back through the walls of the capillaries into the blood system and travel in the blood into wider tubes called veins. The veins carry the blood back to the heart. The heart then pumps this blood through a large artery to the lungs where the carbon dioxide is exchanged for fresh oxygen and the blood is returned to the heart through a vein. The heart gives this oxygen-rich blood another push and sends it out through a large artery around the body again.

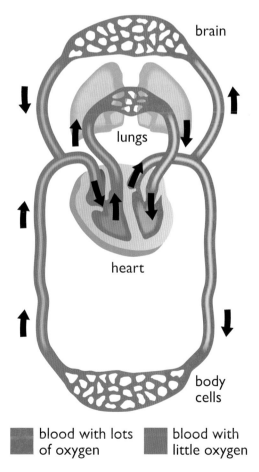

The journey of the blood around the body

To do: Investigate blood flow

You will need:

- timer, clock or watch

Stand up straight with your hands hanging down beside you. Raise one hand in the air, as if you were asking a question in class and keep the other hand beside you. Hold your hand in the air for one minute. Time yourself with a timer or clock. At the end of one minute, hold your hands together in front of you and compare them. Do you notice a difference in their colour?

Try to explain why one hand was paler in colour than the other.

When someone feels faint or dizzy, they may be advised to lie down on the floor. Try to explain why this may help them feel better.

Blood travels around your body from the top of your head to the tips of your toes. As it does so, it circulates between the important organs of your body, absorbing **glucose** and minerals as it goes, carrying these to the body cells, while at the same time absorbing waste products from the cells so that they can be removed from the body.

The heart

The heart is really two separate pumps working alongside each other. One side of the heart receives blood refreshed with oxygen from the lungs and then pumps it strongly on its journey around the body. The other side of the heart receives the blood returning from its journey around the body and pumps it back into the lungs. There are four chambers in the heart, two in each half. On each side the blood enters the heart in an upper chamber called the **atrium**. Below it is a lower chamber or **ventricle**.

When the muscles around the ventricle are relaxed the blood from the atrium flows into the ventricle through a one-way inlet **valve**. When the muscles around the ventricle contract the chamber is squeezed, and the blood is forced out through the outlet valve, into the artery. As the muscle relaxes again, more blood can flow into the chamber through the inlet valve.

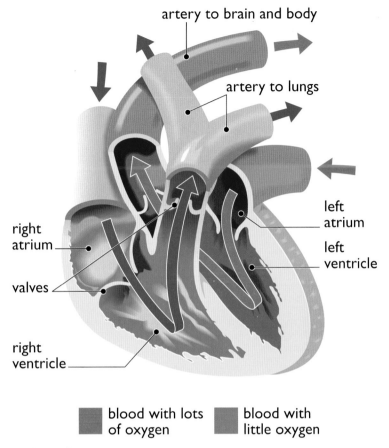

artery to brain and body

artery to lungs

right
atrium

valves

right
ventricle

left
atrium

left
ventricle

blood with lots
of oxygen

blood with
little oxygen

Blood flow through the heart

The valves are important because they keep the blood travelling in the same direction, and prevent it from flowing backwards.

These muscle contractions are called your **heart beat**. The speed at which your heart beats is called your **pulse rate**. Your pulse rate can change. If you are exercising, your heart will beat faster; when you are resting or are asleep your heart will beat more slowly. Your muscles will need more energy when you are exercising so your heart beats faster in order to supply your muscles quickly with the extra oxygen and glucose they need.

To do: Count the beats

You will need:

- timer, clock or watch

1. To find out how fast your heart is beating you will need to find your pulse. Using two fingers gently press on the inside of your other wrist or in your neck, just below the jaw. Move your fingers around until you can feel a pulse beat. This is the speed your heart is pumping your blood through your arteries.

2. Ask your partner to start the timer as you start counting the beats. It is a good idea to close your eyes when counting so that you can concentrate on counting the beats. You partner should tell you to stop when one minute has passed. If you find it easier, count the beats in half a minute and then double it. Your count will tell you how fast your heart is beating in one minute.

3. This is your resting pulse rate. Record this in a table like the one below, writing 'resting' in the activity column and your pulse rate in the second column.

Activity	My pulse rate after the activity, in beats per minute	My partner's pulse rate after the activity, in beats per minute

4. Next, do some exercise, for example running on the spot. Ask your partner to time you doing the activity for two minutes.

5. Now find your pulse again and count the beats in a minute and record your results.

6. Change over and let your partner record their pulse rate before and after the activity.

7. Now try several different activities, for example walking on the spot, lying down and jumping up and down. You should do each activity for two minutes and immediately take your pulse after each activity. Record your results neatly in the table.

8. Now arrange your activities in order starting with the activity with the slowest pulse rate.

Which activity caused your heart to beat the fastest? Look at your partner's results. Which activity caused their heart to beat fastest? Was it the same activity as yours?

If you have time, you might like to investigate what happens to your pulse rate in the 10 minutes or so after you finish exercising. What do you predict you will find?

Think about why it was important that you timed each activity and did it for two minutes each time? Discuss your thoughts with your partner.

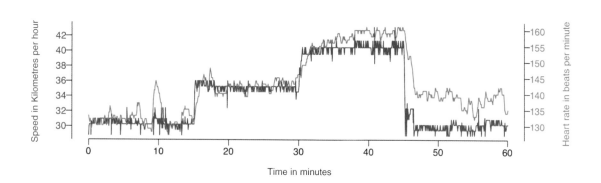

The graph shows how the pulse rate changes as a cyclist works harder to go faster, and slows down

When someone is frightened their heart often pumps faster. Why do you think this is?

To do: Make a heart valve

A valve is like a one-way door. It will only allow the blood to pass through it in one direction. You can make a model to show how this works.

You will need:

- piece of A5 sized card
- 2 pieces of paper each measuring 5 cm by 9 cm
- sticky tape

1. Measure a square 7 cm by 7 cm in the centre of the card. Carefully cut it out and remove it leaving a neat frame.

2. Use sticky tape to stick the two pieces of paper (5 cm by 9 cm) over the hole in your card so that they overlap slightly. They should look like curtains.

3. Hold your frame up so that the side without the curtains is facing you. Now blow gently through your valve. Do the flaps open to let the air through?

4. Turn your frame around, and try to blow through the valve from the other side. What happens this time?

Taking a deep breath

Did you notice that while you were exercising you were breathing faster too? We breathe in to take oxygen from the air and breathe out to get rid of carbon dioxide. When you exercise, your muscles work harder, so they need more oxygen to work properly. The muscles send a message to the brain and the brain makes the heart pump faster. The heart pumps faster sending more blood quickly to the lungs to collect more oxygen. It then rapidly pumps blood carrying fuel and oxygen to the muscles that need it.

A well trained athlete will be able to breathe more deeply and efficiently than an unfit person and will be able to exchange more carbon dioxide for oxygen with each breath. An unfit person taking exercise will therefore need to breathe much faster to take in the oxygen needed.

Breathing difficulties

Some people have difficulty breathing, perhaps because they suffer from diseases such as asthma or bronchitis. Doctors can give inhalers or other medication to help them to breathe more easily.

Other people have difficulty breathing because they have damaged their lungs by **smoking**. Inside the lungs, the air passages are coated with a thick fluid called **mucus**. This helps to keep the air passages moist. Mucus also helps to keep the lungs healthy by washing away bacteria, **viruses** or dust. When people smoke, the cells in the lungs make extra mucus to try to trap the dirt in the smoke. This can cause unpleasant coughing. The cells also become irritated by the smoke and often become swollen, making the tubes in the lungs narrower, and breathing more difficult. Sticky **tar** in the tobacco smoke can also coat the inside of the lungs, making it harder for the oxygen to pass from the air into the blood. Smokers find exercising difficult because they need to breathe much faster to take in all the oxygen they need.

· ·

Exercise 4.4

Use the words in the box to fill in the gaps in the sentences below. Each word may be used once, more than once or not at all.

| veins   capillaries   arteries   blood   heart   oxygen   valves |
| waste   carbon dioxide   exercise   viruses   pulse rate |

1. The _____ is a strong muscle that pumps the _____ around the body.

2. The blood vessels in the body are called _____ , _____ and _____ .

3. _____ carry blood away from the heart.

4. _____ return the blood to the heart.

5. In the lungs _____ is removed from the blood and _____ is absorbed by the blood.

6. The blood carries _____ and glucose to the muscles.

7. The blood also carries _____ products away from the muscles.

8. The heart has _____ which make sure the blood always travels in one direction.

9. When you _____ your heart beats faster.

· ·

Exercise 4.5

1. Explain in your own words why your heart beats faster when you take exercise.

2. Look at the diagram showing the journey of the blood around the body on page 55. Describe the journey in your own words.

3. Explain in your own words how the effects of smoking can restrict your ability to take exercise.

· ·

Taking good care of the amazing human body machine

Exercise

It is important to exercise so that our bodies stay fit and healthy. Exercise keeps our muscles, including the important heart muscle, in good condition and makes them stronger. It also builds up our **stamina** and helps prevent us from becoming overweight or obese. Exercise often makes people feel happier and helps them to sleep better.

Exercise is important to keep our bodies healthy

Smoking

We have already learnt in this chapter how smoking can seriously affect your ability to breathe easily and how it can limit your ability to take exercise. It can also cause disease in the lungs such as **lung cancer** and **emphysema.**

Smoking can also increase the risk of having a **heart attack**. Chemicals in the smoke get into the blood and cause the walls of the arteries to thicken and encourage fat deposits to build up. This means that the heart has to beat harder to push the blood around the body, increasing the likelihood of damage being caused to the heart muscle. If the heart stops beating properly the person may die.

Health warnings on cigarette packets warn people of the dangers of smoking

A chemical called **nicotine** in tobacco smoke is an **addictive drug**. This means that once people have started to smoke, it is very hard for them to give up. The nicotine in cigarettes affects the way the brain works and also damages the heart by causing it to beat harder and faster, putting it under a lot of extra pressure.

Cigarette packets have health warnings printed on them reminding people of the dangers of smoking. There is also a law that stops cigarettes being sold to children. When someone smokes, the smoke from their cigarette can also be breathed in by other people around them. This is called **passive smoking** and can damage the health of these people, especially if they are young children. For this reason, the governments of many countries have now made smoking illegal in public places such as restaurants, buses, trains and offices.

Did you know?
Around the year 1700 the pupils at Eton were punished for not smoking. People thought that smoking prevented them from catching fevers!

Alcohol

Alcohol is another dangerous substance that can cause problems for the human body. Many people drink small quantities of alcohol with a meal or as part of an evening out. In small amounts it does little harm, although it can slow down the speed at which you react to things and if you are driving it will make you more likely to have an accident. Alcohol can also affect your judgement and make you take unnecessary risks. This is why there are strict rules about how much alcohol you may drink if you are going to drive a car.

Drinking alcohol can damage the liver

When people drink too much alcohol they become **drunk**. People who are drunk sometimes become violent and get involved in fights. They lose their sense of balance and often fall and hurt themselves. They may be sick, which is not very pleasant for other people around them. They will also probably feel unwell the following day as their bodies try to remove the alcohol from the blood. In large amounts alcohol can seriously damage the heart, **liver** and stomach and will often cause people to put on weight.

The liver is the organ responsible for removing poisons like alcohol from the blood. Children and young people can very easily damage their livers through drinking, so there is a law preventing sales to children and young people under the age of 18.

Drugs

Drugs are chemicals that affect the body in some way. Nicotine and alcohol are both drugs. Some drugs can be used to protect us from diseases and help the body fight infections. These drugs, usually known as **medicines**, have enabled people to live longer and healthier lives. Medicines are given to us by doctors who have been trained to understand which drugs are safe for us to use and how much is safe for us to take. We must use these medicines carefully, making sure we follow the doctor's instructions, otherwise they could harm us rather than helping us to get better. It is also important never

Medicines are drugs that can help us to fight disease but they must be taken exactly according to doctors' instructions

to take medicines that have been given to someone else. Doctors know how to work out the correct **dose** for each person and what is right for someone else might not be safe for you.

There are other drugs, however, that are not given to people by doctors. Some people find that these drugs, such as heroin or cocaine, make them feel relaxed or excited. They take them even though they know that they can cause serious harm to their bodies. The drugs are addictive and the body becomes dependent on them. The person has to take more and more and they find they cannot stop. These drugs can cause damage to the brain, stomach and liver, and can cause a lot of unhappiness. Most of these drugs are illegal and expensive. **Addicts** need to find the money to buy them but are often too ill to work.

Did you know?
When people take illegal drugs they often use a syringe and a needle to inject them into their bodies. Sometimes these get left lying around and you may find them. They may contain traces of the drugs and have blood on them. If you ever find one of these syringes, you should not touch it. You should tell an adult where it is so that it can be picked up and disposed of safely.

The human body machine will work much better and for much longer without these poisons and harmful substances. Why do you think people start to take these dangerous drugs? How do you think you can protect yourself from a situation where you might be tempted to try them?

Remember that a healthy, balanced diet and plenty of regular exercise are the best ways to keep the human body machine in good working order!

Exercise 4.6

1. What diseases may be caused by smoking?

2. What is meant by the term 'addictive'?

3. What is the name of the addictive chemical in tobacco smoke?

4. Why are there strict rules about how much alcohol a person can drink if they are going to drive a car?

5. Which organ in the body is responsible for removing alcohol from the blood?

6. Describe some of the ways in which people's behaviour may be affected when they drink a lot of alcohol.

7. What is a medicine?

8. Explain why you should never take medicines that have been given to other people.

9. Explain clearly why you should never pick up a syringe and needle if you find them lying around.

Exercise 4.7: Extension question

Write a story about teenagers trying to persuade a child to try smoking. What arguments do you think the child could use to stand up to the teenagers? How would they respond? You could write this as a play script and act it out with your friends.

Chapter 5: Microbes

What are microbes?

Microbes (sometimes known as **micro-organisms**) are very small and are only visible through a microscope. They are everywhere: in the air, water and soil and in our bodies. Some microbes are useful, and some are harmful. There are three main types of microbes: **bacteria, viruses** and **fungi**.

Did you know?
Bacteria were the first living things on Earth. For 2 billion years they were the only living things. They are found in the bodies of almost all living things and in every part of the world, including the ice in the Arctic, in hot springs and in the outer atmosphere.

Microbes and disease

Most common diseases are caused by microbes. Different types of microbe cause different diseases.

Bacteria multiply very quickly in the warm moist conditions of the body and cause diseases such as sore throats, whooping cough, bronchitis, food poisoning and typhoid. They also cause **infections** in wounds.

Viruses are much smaller and cause diseases such as colds, flu, measles, chicken pox and HIV/AIDS.

Fungi can cause diseases on the skin such as athlete's foot and ringworm.

Microbes can get into or onto your body in many different ways. Some microbes are transferred from one person to another through the air. When you cough or sneeze, for example, millions of microbial particles are blown out into the air. These can be breathed in by someone

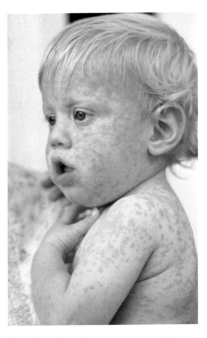

Measles is a disease caused by a virus

else, who then might 'catch' your cold or cough. Some diseases, for example chicken pox, are transferred by touching someone who has the disease.

Microbes are also passed from one person to another by poor **hygiene**. If someone uses the toilet and forgets to wash their hands or sneezes into their hands, there will be microbes on them which will then be transferred to anything they touch. The microbes can then be picked up by other people.

Some diseases are spread by animals. For example, flies that lay their eggs in the rotting remains of dead animals can transfer the bacteria that they pick up on their feet to other places. This is why it is best to prevent flies landing on your food. Other diseases are spread through dirty water. Microbes in drinking water can cause diarrhoea, which is the most common cause of death in young children in some places in the world.

Did you know?

Cholera is a disease that spreads rapidly. It has caused the deaths of millions of people throughout history. Until the 19th century no one knew how it was caused. In 1853–1854 an outbreak of cholera in London killed more than 10,000 people. John Snow, a doctor, marked on a map where the people who caught the disease lived. He showed that the disease had probably come from a water pump in Broad Street. In those days, most people did not

have a water supply in their homes and all water had to be collected from a pump or well. He persuaded the authorities to take the handle off the pump so that no one could use it. Once people started using different sources of water the number of cases dropped rapidly, showing that the disease had been spread through the water. John Snow suggested that it was a microbe that had caused the disease.

This was not proven until 1885, when a German scientist, Robert Koch, identified the bacteria that cause cholera. Although it is now possible to prevent cholera by providing clean drinking water and by **vaccination** (see page 74), people still die from the disease in some parts of the world.

Exercise 5.1

Use the words in the box to complete the following sentences. Each word may be used once, more than once or not at all.

bacteria colds small helpful touch fungi microscope harmful viruses air flu drinking water infection

1. Microbes are very _____ and can only be seen using a _____ .

2. Some microbes are _____ to us, but some are _____ .

3. There are three types of microbes: _____ , _____ and _____ .

4. Diseases such as sore throats, typhoid and cholera are caused by _____ .

5. Viruses cause diseases such as _____ and _____ .

6. Diseases caused by microbes can be spread in _____ _____ , in the _____ or by _____ .

Exercise 5.2

1. Explain in your own words what is meant by the term 'microbe'.

2. Give another name for microbes.

3. Name the three main groups of microbes.

4. Name three diseases that are caused by bacteria.

5. Name three diseases that are caused by viruses.

6. Describe in your own words the main ways in which diseases can be passed from one person to another.

7. (a) What was the name of the 19th century doctor who proved that cholera was spread in drinking water?

   (b) How did he prove his theory?

8. Name the German scientist who discovered the bacterium that causes cholera.

What can be done to help?

There are many ways of making sure that people do not catch diseases. Some of them are simple, for example washing your hands after using the toilet and before each meal. If you have been playing outside or handling animals you should wash your hands to remove the harmful microbes and stop them from getting into your body through your mouth. If you cut yourself, you should clean the wound carefully and cover it to prevent bacteria from getting in and causing an infection. If you have exercised and you have got a bit hot and sweaty, you should wash your body properly.

Washing hands helps to stop diseases being passed from one person to another

Washing removes the bacteria that cause unpleasant smells and also helps to stop the fungal infections that can occur on your skin.

If you have a cold or a cough, it is important that you try not to pass on the virus to other people. Putting a hand across your mouth when you cough can stop many virus particles being blown out into the air. If you have a cold, you can sneeze and blow your nose into a tissue and then throw the tissue away. The microbes will then be placed where they cannot infect someone else. It is a good idea to wash your hands more often when you have a cough or cold.

To do: Pass the microbe

You will need:

- glitter
- plastic sandwich bag
- dry cloth or duster
- soap, water and towels
- dish cloth

1. Put some glitter into the sandwich bag. Squeeze the air out carefully and seal the top and then rub the bag with the dry cloth or duster. The glitter represents microbes. Rubbing the bag like this will make a static electric charge which makes the glitter stick to things more easily.

2. Open the bag and ask one person to put their hand into the bag and rub it around a bit. This will cover the hand with glitter 'microbes', just as if the person had sneezed into their hand.

3. Ask that person to go around the class and shake hands with about four or five people. Then ask them to count how many glitter 'microbes' they can see on their hands.

4. These people could then shake hands with some more people. How many glitter 'microbes' are passed on this time? How many handshakes does it take before no particles are passed on? How many people have been 'infected' with the glitter 'disease'?

5. Now ask everyone to wash their hands. Some could just run their hands under running water and some could do the job properly, rubbing their hands thoroughly with soap. They should then dry their hands on a towel. Now look at the hands again. How many glitter 'microbes' are there still on the hands? Does it make a difference how they washed them? How many 'microbes' have finished up on the towel?

6. Next take the dish cloth and make it a bit damp before putting it in the bag and shaking it around a bit. You now have a 'dirty' dish cloth.

7. Try wiping some tables with the dish cloth. How many glitter 'microbes' end up on the table? Do you think that a table wiped with a dirty dish cloth is cleaner or dirtier than it was before being wiped? How could we prevent diseases being passed around in this way?

If you get a bacterial infection such as a sore throat or a chest infection, your doctor may give you a type of **medicine** called an **antibiotic**. The first antibiotic was called **penicillin**. It was discovered by mistake when a Scottish scientist called Alexander Fleming, who was studying bacteria, was a little careless about cleaning his apparatus. When he looked at one of the dirty dishes he noticed that a type of fungus called a **mould** was growing in the dish, and it seemed to have killed off the bacteria around it. Three other scientists, an Australian called Howard Florey, a German called Ernst Chain and an Englishman

Alexander Fleming

called Norman Heatley developed a medicine using the mould. This medicine was vital in the Second World War when it helped to cure infections in the wounds of injured soldiers and saved many lives.

Antibiotics are good at fighting bacterial diseases but cannot help with diseases caused by viruses. This is why your doctor will not give you an antibiotic when you have a cold or flu. Because these diseases are caused by viruses the medicine will not work. So, how can we treat viral disease? There are some medicines that may help but they do not work for all viral diseases and they are not always very effective. With most viral diseases, the only thing we can do is to wait for the body's own disease-fighting system, the **immune system**, to fight the disease. The best thing to do is to try to prevent people from getting the disease in the first place. One way to do this is by a process called **vaccination**.

Vaccination helps to prevent diseases caused by viruses

When you were a baby, you almost certainly had some **injections**. You may also have had some since then, perhaps when you were going on holiday. These injections, known as vaccinations, work by putting a tiny bit of the disease or dead virus particles into your body. Your body recognises these as being dangerous and your immune system makes special chemicals called **antibodies** in your blood. These attach themselves to the virus and remove it from your body. After they have cleaned up the virus they remain in your blood ready to fight that virus if it enters your body again. Some scientists, called **biochemists**, are always working to make new **vaccines** to fight diseases caused by viruses. Some diseases are now very rare, especially in developed countries, as a result of vaccinations.

Exercise 5.3

1. Explain why it is important to wash your hands before a meal.

2. Suggest at least three other times when it is a good idea to wash your hands.

3. When you have a cold how can you avoid passing your cold to other people?

4. (a) Name the type of medicine that can be used to cure diseases caused by bacteria.

   (b) Describe briefly in your own words how this type of medicine was discovered.

   (c) Why is this type of medicine not given to people with colds or flu?

5. What is another name for a vaccination?

6. Explain in your own words how vaccinations help your body to fight diseases caused by viruses.

. . . .

Edward Jenner and smallpox

One disease that is now completely extinct is smallpox. This is the disease that led to the invention of vaccinations as a method of disease prevention.

Edward Jenner (1749–1823) was a doctor who lived in Gloucestershire. In the 18th century, smallpox was quite a common disease causing lots of blister-like spots to appear on the skin. The disease was easily passed from one person to another through touch. It killed many people, but the people who survived were left with scars, called pock-marks, especially on their faces. Edward Jenner saw many people with this terrible disease and he wanted to help them.

It was generally known that milkmaids, the girls responsible for milking cows, very rarely caught smallpox. Edward Jenner wondered why this might be. He visited farms where these girls worked and saw that the cows sometimes developed a disease called cowpox. This was a bit like smallpox because the cows developed blister-like spots on their udders, but it did not make the cows ill. Jenner found that the milkmaids were infected with cowpox as they milked the cows. He thought perhaps this was protecting them from smallpox.

In 1796, to test his theory, he collected some **fluid** from the blisters on the skin of a milkmaid with cowpox. He then made a small cut on the arm of an eight-year old boy, called James Phipps and rubbed the cowpox fluid into the cut. After a while he tried to infect James with smallpox but the boy remained quite healthy. This suggested that the cowpox infection had prevented him from getting smallpox. Jenner called the process vaccination, from the Latin word *vacca*, meaning 'cow'.

Jenner repeated the experiment with several other children, including his own baby son, but it took some time before this strange new idea was widely accepted. The process was so successful, however, that smallpox no longer infects people in any country.

. . . .

Exercise 5.4

Use the words in the box to complete the following sentences. Each word may be used once, more than once or not at all.

| London   cowpox   vaccination   James   Gloucestershire |
| smallpox   extinct   milkmaids   children   Reginald   antibodies |

1. Edward Jenner was a doctor who lived in _____ .

2. Jenner wanted to stop people getting a disease called _____ .

3. He noticed that _____ did not get the disease and he thought that this might be because they caught _____ from the cows.

4. Jenner put some fluid from the cowpox blisters into the arm of a boy called _____ Phipps.

5. Later he tried to infect the boy with _____ but he did not get the disease.

6. He tried the experiment again with some other _____ and they did not get the disease either.

7. Jenner called this method of preventing disease _____ .

8. This process has been so successful that smallpox is now an _____ disease.

Exercise 5.5: Extension question

Read the story of the invention of vaccination again. Imagine that you are either Edward Jenner, James Phipps or James Phipps's mother. How do you think they felt? Tell the story again in your own words from the viewpoint of your chosen character. You could do this in the form of a letter or a diary or maybe as a conversation between your character and someone else.

To do: More microbe history

Have you ever been in a hospital? If so, you will know how important hygiene is in modern hospitals. Visitors are often asked to clean their hands with special anti-bacterial cleansers and nurses and doctors wash their hands before they visit each patient. It has not always been like this. Before scientists discovered how microbes cause infections and disease, many people died, especially if they were having an operation.

The oldest operating theatre in the world is in the church next to St Thomas's Hospital, London

Use books or the internet to find out about operating theatres in the 19th century. Look at how they are different to modern operating theatres and how the work of Joseph Lister contributed to the improvement in hospital hygiene. You could do a little project, or design a poster or a wall display about this.

Microbes can also cause disease when they get into food. It is important that kitchen surfaces are kept clean and that food is stored properly and cooked properly to prevent these microbes infecting people. Many foods are easily spoilt by microbes. 'Use by' dates are printed on the packaging to help people make sure they are still safe to eat.

Not all bad

However, not all microbes are bad. In fact, there are more helpful microbes than there are harmful ones. Some carry out useful jobs in the body, and others are useful in the production of foods and drinks. Some microbes are decomposers and help break down dead material, returning nutrients to the soil. Other microbes break down the material in sewage tanks so that clean water can be returned to reservoirs and rivers.

Microbes are used to clean the water in sewage works

Did you know?
You have millions of microbes, mostly bacteria, living inside your intestines. These microbes help to keep you healthy in many ways. They help to digest food, produce useful vitamins in the gut and they help keep your immune system healthy. They also help to fight harmful bacteria that might cause disease.

Many of the foods you like to eat are made using microbes. Bacteria are used to make yoghurt and cheese from milk. 'Blue' cheese has ripples of mould, a type of fungus, running through it. **Yeast**, another type of fungus, is used to make bread and, in the process called **brewing**, it is used to make alcoholic drinks such as wine and beer. Cocoa beans are also treated to allow bacteria to work on them before they can be made into chocolate.

Yeast is a very useful fungus. When bread is made, yeast is usually added to the dough. The dough is then left in a warm place for a while. In these warm, damp conditions, the yeast begins to carry out respiration, feeding on the carbohydrates in the dough and creating carbon dioxide. Bubbles of carbon dioxide are trapped in the stretchy bread dough and make the dough rise. When the bread is cooked, the dough becomes drier and more solid so the bubbles are held firmly, making a delicious, light bread.

Did you know?
Bread made without yeast is often called unleavened bread. At the Jewish festival called Passover, unleavened bread is eaten as part of a special meal called the Seder.

Unleavened bread is part of the Seder or Passover meal

To make wine, yeast is mixed with water and the juice from fruit, usually grapes. The yeast feeds on the sugars in the fruit juice and begins to carry out respiration. Carbon dioxide is produced and begins to bubble up through the liquid and into the air. As it feeds on the sugars, the yeast also produces alcohol. This process is called **fermentation**. Wine has been made in this way for thousands of years and beer is made in a similar process.

Before clean drinking water was available to everyone in the UK, many people drank beer or wine rather than water because the brewing process killed off the bacteria in the water. Beer and wine were therefore safer to drink than water.

To do: Investigate yeast

You will need:

- spatula
- dried yeast
- beakers, test tubes or other containers
- sugar
- water

Dried yeast is in a state where it is inactive and not respiring. We say that it is **dormant**. To activate it, it needs to be mixed with water. If the conditions are right, the yeast will begin to respire and make bubbles of carbon dioxide. In this investigation you will try to find out what conditions are best to encourage the yeast to respire.

1. Place a small quantity (about 1 spatula scoop) of dried yeast in a beaker, add about two spatula scoops of sugar and cover with warm water. Leave this mixture for a while in a warm place and see what changes happen.

2. Discuss the conditions you gave the yeast to make these changes that occur. What do you predict will happen if you change each of these conditions? For example, at what temperature was the mixture? What do you think would happen if the temperature were lower or higher?

3. Choose one variable (condition) to investigate and design a fair test to find out what value is best for the yeast. For example, you might try to find out what temperature is best or whether the amount of sugar added makes a difference. Remember to think about what you will need to keep the same for each of your tests. How many tests will you carry out? What values of your chosen variable will you choose to use? How will you measure your result?

4. Carry out your investigation and record your results carefully in a table. Discuss your results with other groups. Maybe other groups have chosen to investigate the same variable as you did. If so, do your results agree? If they do not agree, can you suggest why? If other groups have done different investigations, you can put all the results together to come to an overall conclusion about the best conditions for yeast to respire.

Exercise 5.6

1. Name some foods that are made using microbes.

2. Some bacteria and fungi can be described as decomposers. How are these microbes helpful in the environment?

3. Why are the microbes in your gut so important?

4. (a) Which type of microbe is added to dough to make bread rise?

   (b) Describe in your own words how the activity of this microbe causes bread to rise.

5. What name is given to bread made without the microbe you named in question 4?

6. What is meant by the term 'fermentation'?

7. How is wine made?

8. Why did many people in medieval times drink wine or beer rather than water?

Chapter 6: Separating mixtures

Mixtures are all around us

What is a mixture? A **mixture** is just two or more things mixed together. For scientists, however, mixtures are very important and can pose some interesting scientific challenges.

Let's start by thinking about mixtures you may be familiar with. Sometimes it is easy to see that things are mixed together. For example, the grains, nuts and fruit in a bowl of muesli can be seen clearly and it would be quite easy to pick out each of the different foods to separate the mixture.

Sometimes, though, it is not possible to see the individual **components** of the mixture. For example, it is not possible to see the sugar in a sugar solution. In fact, the mixture looks like **pure** water.

Air is a mixture of gases. Most of the air is a gas called **nitrogen** and it is mixed with **oxygen**. It also contains much smaller amounts of **carbon dioxide**, water vapour and other gases, for example, argon.

Sea water is a mixture of water and several different **salts**. Among these are common or table salt, which chemists call **sodium chloride**, and which makes the water taste salty. The water also contains microscopic animal and plant material called **plankton** and possibly mud, sand, shell fragments and bits of seaweed. Often sea water is **polluted** with material that we have added to it. This could be waste from factories, chemicals washed into the sea from farmland or even sewage.

All of these are mixtures. Now let's think scientifically about them. Do you think the mixture of gases that makes up the air is always the same? What might change the mixture? For example, is the air you breathe in the same as the air you breathe out? In what ways might it be different? Can you think of any other ways in which the mixture that we call air might change? What about sea water? Is all sea water the same?

Did you know?
The water in the Dead Sea, a huge salt water lake between Israel and Jordan, is more than eight times as salty as the big oceans. The huge amount of salt makes the water very dense and people can float easily in the water. The Dead Sea is the lowest place on Earth at roughly 400 metres below sea level.

As we stated earlier, a mixture is made up of two or more things mixed together, but the really interesting thing about mixtures is that they can change but still be mixtures. For example, the air we breathe out contains less oxygen, more carbon dioxide and more water vapour than the air we breathe in but we happily call both of them 'air'.

To do: Think of some more mixtures

Work with a partner or in a small group. See how many examples of mixtures you can think of and write them down. Then think about how these mixtures might change or be changed by natural events or by human actions.

You should be able to think of quite a number of mixtures, as pure substances are quite unusual. Almost everything contains at least a little bit of something else, either deliberately or by chance. For example, you may think that the water you drink is pure but it almost certainly isn't. Our drinking water contains dissolved chemicals that give it some taste, so it is probably a good thing that the water is not pure. If you tasted water from different parts of the country, or maybe different countries, you might be able to taste the difference.

To do: Investigate different waters

Water from different places is different. Your teacher will give you some water samples to investigate. You may have some sea water, pond water, tap water, **distilled** (pure) water or some mineral water.

For this activity you will need:

- sheet of rigid clear plastic
- sheet of black paper
- water samples
- **pipettes** (one for each water sample)
- sticky labels (one for each water sample)

1. Place the sheet of plastic on top of the sheet of black paper in a place that is warm but not windy and where no one will knock it by mistake.

2. Use the pipettes to put a little 'puddle', about 1 cm across, of each water onto your sheet of plastic and label each puddle. Try to make all the puddles the same size. Then leave your sheet alone until all the water has dried up (**evaporated**).

3. Explain why it is important to have one pipette for each type of water.

4. Try to predict what you will find when the water has dried up. Explain your ideas to your partner. Record your predictions and final observations in a table like the one below:

Water sample	Prediction	Final observation

Exercise 6.1

Use the words from the box to complete the following sentences. Each word may be used once, more than once or not at all.

> pure   gases   sodium   oxygen   mixture   nitrogen   distilled

1. A _____ is made up of two or more things mixed together.

2. Air is a mixture of _____.

3. Most of the air is made from _____ and this gas is mixed with _____ and some other gases.

4. The name that chemists give to table salt is _____ chloride.

5. Our drinking water is not _____ water because it contains dissolved salts.

. . . .

Exercise 6.2

1. What materials may be present in the mixture we call sea water?

2. Describe how you could show that sea water contains more dissolved materials than tap water.

3. Where is the Dead Sea?

4. Why is it especially easy to float in the Dead Sea?

5. What is special about the position of the Dead Sea?

. . . .

Separating mixtures

Scientists often need to separate different parts of a mixture. Chemists often want to obtain pure chemicals for their experiments. These chemicals almost always start as part of a mixture so we need to be able to separate the mixtures to obtain pure substances. There are many other reasons why people might want to separate a mixture and there are lots of different separation methods. We are going to learn about some of them in this chapter and more later on.

A stirring rod makes it easier to pour without making a mess

Decanting

Decanting is probably the simplest way of separating a mixture. It works for a mixture containing a liquid and pieces of a solid that will sink quickly to the bottom of the container. You **decant** the liquid by pouring it carefully into another container, leaving the solid material, sometimes called a **sediment**, behind. Pouring can be made easier by holding a stirring rod by the spout of the beaker, so the liquid trickles down the stirring rod rather than dribbling down the side of the beaker and making a mess.

Did you know?

Sometimes bottles of wine contain solid materials that would not be very pleasant to drink. If the wine is left to stand for a while the sediment sinks to the bottom and then the wine can be decanted into another container. These containers are often called decanters.

Wine can be poured into a decanter to remove the sediment before drinking

A sieve is useful for separating large pieces from a mixture

Sieving

You may have used a **sieve** in the kitchen at home. A sieve is a special tool to help separate mixtures. The mixture often contains a liquid, usually water, and large pieces of something insoluble, such as vegetables. You may also have used a sieve to separate out the lumps in some flour when making a cake. Scientists sometimes use sieves too. When investigating your soil samples in Chapter 8 you could use a stack of soil sieves.

Filtering

Sieving is only useful for removing large particles from a mixture because sieves have quite large holes. They don't work if the insoluble material is in very small particles. The small particles of solid could pass through the holes in a sieve. They may float around in the liquid, giving it an opaque or milky appearance. We call this type of mixture a **suspension**.

To separate a suspension, we need a special kind of sieve with really tiny holes, so small we cannot see them. They need to be large enough for the water particles to go through but small enough to stop particles of solid passing through. This kind of sieve is called a **filter** and is often made from a special type of paper called filter paper. To filter a mixture we fold the filter paper and put it into a funnel and then pour the mixture through it. The liquid will pass through the paper but the larger, insoluble material will get stuck in the paper. We call this the **residue**. The liquid that passes through the paper is called the **filtrate**.

Step 1: Fold in half.

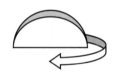

Step 2: Fold into quarters.

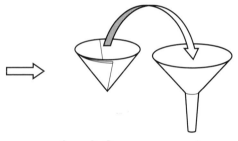

Step 3: Open out to make a cone shape with three layers on one side and one layer on the other.

Apparatus for filtering

Evaporating

Decanting, sieving and filtering will only work if you are separating out pieces of an insoluble material. When you are dealing with a soluble material you need a different process. A soluble material is one where the substance dissolves. The crystals break up into such tiny particles that they can pass through the holes in filter paper, so they will remain mixed with the liquid in the filtrate. So we cannot use filtering to separate a **solute** (dissolved substance) from a **solution**.

We know that evaporation is the process of a liquid turning into a gas or vapour. When you investigated the water samples (on page 84) you allowed the water to evaporate and so separated the mixture of water and dissolved material in the samples. When the water, the **solvent**, evaporated it became mixed with gases in the air but the dissolved materials in the water, the solutes, were left behind.

Evaporation is often used in science. Scientists quite often need to obtain dry samples of chemicals from solutions. You can do this by allowing the solvent to evaporate slowly, as you did with the water samples, but this can take a long time. We can speed up the process by heating the mixture gently. You can do this by placing it near a radiator, on a hot plate or, if you have the right apparatus, using the method shown in the picture.

It is very important to remember never to go on heating the solution until it is completely dry. If you do, the hot, solid material may start to spit out and could hurt you. You could also heat the material too much and this might change it in some way. You should always stop heating when there is still a little moisture in the container and allow the last little bit of solvent to evaporate by itself.

Evaporating a solution

Exercise 6.3

1. What is the meaning of the term 'solvent'?

2. In a solution of salt in water, which of the substances is the solute?

3. What is a suspension?

4. Which separation method would be best for separating the following mixtures:

   (a) water and gravel

   (b) a solution of salt in water

   (c) a suspension of powdered chalk in water

5. Explain why you could not separate the salts out of sea water by filtering.

6. When evaporating a solution, why should you not heat it until it is completely dry?

7. If you filtered a mixture of soil and water, which material would become the residue?

To do: The rock salt challenge

Rock salt is the material spread on icy roads in winter. It contains salt, which makes the ice melt more easily, and pieces of sand and grit, which increase friction so that cars do not slide around so much. Rock salt is a mixture. You can read more about rock salt later in this chapter.

Your teacher will give you a sample of rock salt. Your challenge is to separate the mixture so that you finish up with two piles: one of clean white salt and the other of sand and grit.

You will need to use more than one of the methods that you have learnt about in this chapter. You will also need to think about what you learnt in *Junior Science Book 2* about soluble and insoluble materials and making solutions.

You should plan your method and ask your teacher to check it before you start the experiment. Remember to think about safety. What precautions do you need to take in order to keep yourself and others safe?

How we can use separation

Common salt

Common salt, usually known simply as salt, is a very important chemical. It is an essential part of the diet of most animals, including humans, and for many centuries it was an important way of preserving foods, especially meat. Salt was a very valuable material. Countries that had a lot of salt used it to trade with countries that did not have a supply of their own. For example, the Egyptians traded salt for things such as timber and glass. Long caravans of camels carried salt across the Sahara desert right up until the late 20th century.

Salt can be obtained by evaporating sea water

Common salt can be obtained from two main sources. The first is the sea. In hot countries, sea water can be contained in shallow areas called **lagoons** or **salt pans**. The water then evaporates in the sun and the salt is left behind.

In cooler countries, such as Britain, there is not enough sunshine to make this method possible. Instead, sea water is filtered and then heated to evaporate the water. If salt solution is allowed to dry slowly, salt crystals begin to form in lovely cube or pyramid shapes. If a crystal of salt is allowed to grow for a long time it develops into a large cube.

The second source of salt is salt mines. Millions of years ago some places that are now dry land were under the water of tropical oceans. As these oceans dried up, their salt was left behind in thick layers. These layers became covered in sediments of sand and silt to become an area of sedimentary rock. The rocks were then lifted by the movement of the Earth's crust and so the salt is now found in these rocks on dry land. (See *Junior Science Book 1*, Chapter 3 for more information about rocks.) This rock salt is mined

Salt forms cube-shaped crystals

using huge grinding machines and is crushed for use on the roads and for other industrial processes. Some of it is also **purified** for eating, using a very large-scale version of the method that you will have used when separating your sample of rock salt.

Did you know?
Someone has estimated that if all the oceans and salt lakes in the world dried up, there would be enough salt left behind to build a wall 180 miles tall and one mile thick all around the equator. That's a lot of salt!

Salt can also be mined from rocks as in the Winsford Rock Salt Mines, Cheshire
Photograph by kind permission of Paul Deakin, Matthews & Son LLP

Oil chemicals

Oil is formed from the remains of tiny sea creatures. Millions of years ago, when they died and fell to the bottom of the sea they became covered with layers of sand and silt. The heat and pressure of the sand and silt then changed the chemicals that made up the bodies of the animals into the chemicals that make up the mixture we call oil.

The oil we pump from the ground through oil wells is not very useful in its natural state. It contains hundreds of different chemicals mixed together. Some are very thick and sticky, such as the tar we use for road surfaces. Some are very light liquids that evaporate easily, such as the petrol we put into cars, and some are gases. There are many different products that can be obtained from oil. These different products are separated using a

In an oil refinery, oil can be separated to give useful products

process called fractional distillation. This takes place at oil refineries. You will learn more about this process later but at a simple level it involves heating the mixture very carefully. Different chemicals evaporate at different temperatures because they all have different boiling points (see *Junior Science Book 2*, Chapter 3). This makes it possible to separate them.

Oil is important to us because it provides many products that we take for granted. There is oil for heating, diesel and petrol for cars and lorries and aviation **fuel** for aircraft. Chemicals from oil are used to make plastics, candles, clothing and paint, as **lubricants** to keep machinery working smoothly and for many other things as well.

Unfortunately, we are using up oil very quickly and the time will come when these products will no longer be readily available because oil will be so scarce. One of the big challenges for chemists is to find new ways of providing all these products using materials that will not run out. One example of this could be **bio-fuels.** These are fuels made from plant material that can be used in vehicles instead of petrol or diesel. This could be one answer to the problem. However, we will need to find ways of growing enough plant material to make this fuel without cutting down forests or taking up land that is needed to grow food. Products that can be made from materials that are replaceable and do not harm the environment or endanger our well-being are described as **sustainable**.

Chemists and material scientists are very important people. Without them we would struggle to find new, sustainable ways of making the things that we need without using oil. Maybe you will be one of these important scientists when you grow up!

Exercise 6.4

Use words from the box to complete the sentences on the next page. Each word may be used once, more than once or not at all.

timber	sea	plastics	preserve	glass	cook	hundreds
petrol	mines	meat	millions	liquids	fuel	

1. Common salt was once used to _____ food, especially _____.

2. The Egyptians traded salt for products such as _____ and _____.

3. Common salt can be obtained from the _____ or from _____.

4. Oil was formed from the bodies of tiny _____ creatures that died _____ of years ago.

5. Chemicals from oil are used to make products such as _____ and _____.

. . . .

Exercise 6.5

1. Explain why common salt was so valuable to people in past centuries.

2. (a) Describe how salt can be obtained from the sea in hot countries.
    (b) How is sea salt obtained in Britain?

3. Salt mines contain layers of salt in between layers of rock. Explain how these layers of salt were formed.

4. Describe in your own words how oil is formed.

5. Name some products that we obtain from oil.

6. What name is given to the process used in oil refineries to separate the chemicals in oil?

7. Why do scientists need to look for alternatives to oil?

8. What is bio-fuel?

9. What is meant by the term 'sustainable'?

10. What do we have to do to make sure that bio-fuel is produced in a sustainable way?

Exercise 6.6: Extension questions

Joe and Laura are given a mixture by their teacher. The mixture contains the following materials: wax pellets, powdered charcoal, salt and iron filings. They are also given a sieve with holes 2 mm in diameter, some beakers, some water, a funnel and filter paper and a magnet.

1. Copy and complete the following table to show the properties of the four things in the mixture.

Material	Is it soluble?	Are the pieces larger than 2 mm?	Is it magnetic?	Does it float on water?
wax pellets		yes		yes
powdered charcoal		no		
salt		no		
iron filings		no		

2. Suggest a method that Joe and Laura could use in order to separate all four of the materials in their mixture.

. . . .

Drawing science diagrams

When scientists record the way they carry out an experiment, they often need to show the apparatus they have used. One way of doing this might be to take a photograph but sometimes photographs are not very clear and it is difficult to avoid getting all sorts of extra things in the background.

The clearest way is to draw a **diagram**. Diagrams are not pictures. We do not try to draw our apparatus in 3D because it is difficult to do so clearly unless you are a very good artist. Instead, we use a simplified set of shapes to show the different pieces of apparatus.

You should always use a sharp pencil and a ruler when drawing these diagrams.

Your diagrams should not be too small, as it is hard to make tiny diagrams clear enough, nor too large. Your teacher will help you to get the size right.

The really important thing is to make them neat and clear. Here are the shapes that we use for the apparatus you may have used in this chapter.

This is how we draw a beaker. Notice that there is no line across the top. The beaker also has a flat base, always drawn using a ruler, but has curved corners.

This is how we draw a funnel. Notice again that there is no line across the top and also that there is no line across the bottom of the spout.

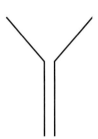

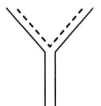

To show the filter paper in the funnel, we draw a v-shape using a dashed line.

You may have supported your funnel in a conical flask. This is how you draw a conical flask.

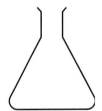

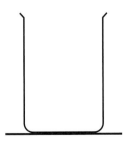

Remember to draw both the bottom of the beaker and the surface it is resting on

There are some things that we do not bother to draw because they are not important. For instance, we need to show that our apparatus is resting on a flat surface. However, it really doesn't matter whether that flat surface is a table, a laboratory bench or the floor so we do not bother to draw these; we just draw a single straight line, using a ruler, under our diagram.

We do not draw clamps or filter rings either. All that matters is to show that the apparatus is supported in some way. It is not important what is supporting it. You could even be holding it yourself. We show the support with two neat crosses at the sides of the apparatus where the support is gripping it.

We do not draw heaters or Bunsen burners in diagrams. When we want to show that something is being heated we can do this by drawing a neat triangle or an arrow under it with the word 'HEAT' written neatly below it. Some people like to do this with a thin red pen or sharp red crayon but your teacher will tell you how you should do it.

The other thing that we do not draw is you! There is no science diagram shape for a person, so don't try to draw yourself in the diagram.

Diagrams should always be labelled. You do not need to label everything – just enough to make it clear. If you have drawn your diagram neatly and properly, it is probably not necessary to label the obvious things like a beaker. Labels should be written neatly at the side of the diagram to stop them from cluttering up your nice neat drawing. Then use a pencil and a ruler to draw a straight line from the label to the correct part of the diagram.

We can now put all these things together to show how the apparatus was used to filter a mixture:

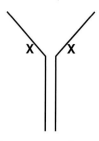

Supports such as clamps are shown by two small neat crosses

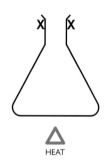

A heater or burner can be shown by a small triangle

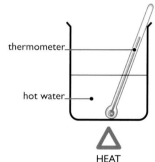

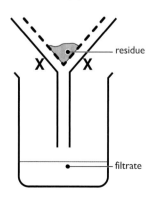

or

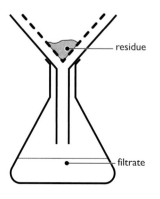

Exercise 6.7: Diagram drawing practice

1. Make neat copies of the diagrams for the following apparatus:

   (a) a beaker

   (b) a funnel with filter paper in it

   (c) a conical flask

2. Now practise drawing the same diagrams without copying them.

3. Draw a neat, labelled diagram of an arrangement of apparatus that you could use to separate a mixture of chalk powder and water by filtering.

· ·

Chromatography

The term **chromatography** comes from the Greek words for colour and writing. Chromatography is a method used to separate a mixture of chemicals that are all dissolved and mixed together, such as the mixture of **dyes** used to make coloured inks. There are a number of different ways of carrying out chromatography. Some require expensive machines and some are quite simple. The method you will use is one of the simple ones and is called **paper chromatography**.

Any **absorbent** paper can be used for chromatography but filter paper or special chromatography paper works best.

To do: Separate coloured inks

You will need:

- a strip of filter paper or chromatography paper
- a pencil
- a coloured felt pen
- a test tube
- some water

1. Draw a line in pencil across the paper, about 1.5 cm up from the bottom.

To do: Separate coloured inks (continued)

2. Use the felt pen to draw a circle of ink on the pencil line, about the size of a pea.

3. Put about 1 cm depth of water in the test tube. Check that the ink circle is above the water level when you put the paper strip into the test tube. This is important because, if the ink is submerged in the water, it will be washed away into the water and there will be none left on the paper for you to test.

4. Drop the strip of paper carefully into the test tube and watch what happens as the liquid soaks into the paper.

5. When the water level nearly reaches the top of the paper, take it out and let it dry. It is now called a **chromatogram**. Can you see which colours of ink were mixed together when making your felt pen?

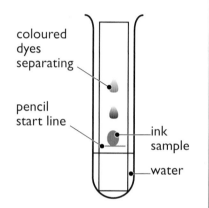

coloured dyes separating

pencil start line

ink sample

water

When you put the paper strip into the water in the experiment above, you will have noticed that the water was quickly absorbed by the paper. The water level rose up the paper and carried the colours with it. Each colour travelled a different distance and so they became separated.

How does this work? When the bottom of the paper is submerged in the water, it becomes very wet. The water is absorbed and gradually moves up, higher and higher up the paper. The soluble inks dissolve in the water and are carried up the paper. Higher up the paper, the amount of water in the paper gets less and less. Gradually the coloured dyes get left behind. The more soluble the dye, the further it is carried up the paper. Any dye that is not soluble in water will not move at all. It will remain in the place where you drew the dot. You should now be able to look at your chromatogram and work out which dye was the most soluble and which was the least soluble.

The base line on a chromatogram must be drawn in pencil because, if you drew it in ink, the dyes making that ink would travel up the paper with the dyes from the felt pen dot and spoil your chromatogram.

Comparing mixtures

Sometimes it is useful to be able to compare the colours in two or more samples. For instance, an art historian could compare the paints used in a mystery picture with those used by one or two known artists in order to help decide who may have painted the mystery picture. It is sometimes useful for detectives to be able to compare paint or ink samples when trying to solve a crime.

In order to compare two or more samples, we need to make a chromatogram of all the samples on one piece of paper. We can then carry out a chromatography experiment just as we did before. When we compare the samples on the chromatogram, we look to see if there are any patches of the same colour that have travelled the same distance up the paper in each of the samples. If this happens, there is a good chance that the dye used was the same one.

To do: Compare felt pen inks

You will need:

- pencil
- ruler
- rectangle of filter paper or chromatography paper that fits into the beaker without touching the sides
- 4 felt pens (you could choose four different colours or you could choose to compare the inks in four pens of the same colour but made by different manufacturers)
- sticky tape
- beaker
- water

1. Using the pencil and ruler, draw a straight line about 1.5 cm up from the bottom of the paper. This must be level so that all the dyes start at the same place and have the same distance to travel up the paper.

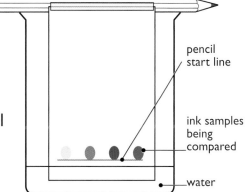

pencil
start line

ink samples being compared

water

To do: Compare felt pen inks (continued)

2. Draw and colour in a pea-sized circle using each of the coloured pens on the pencil line. Try to space them out evenly.

3. Use the sticky tape to stick the top of the paper to the pencil. Rest the pencil across the top of the beaker. Check that the paper hangs down into the beaker so that it almost reaches the bottom of the beaker and does not touch the sides.

4. Take the pencil and paper off the beaker, pour about 1 cm depth of water into the beaker and then replace the pencil and paper. Check that the bottom of the paper is in the water but the water level is below the pencil line.

5. Leave the beaker alone until the water level has risen nearly to the top, then take the paper out and leave your chromatogram to dry.

6. When the paper has dried look carefully at the patches of ink. What coloured dyes were used to make each of the felt pen inks? Can you identify any dyes that are the same in two or more felt pens? Are there any dyes that are in all the inks?

In the experiments you have done, you have used water as the solvent. Some dyes, for example in waterproof ('permanent') marker pens, or some of the **pigments** in flowers and leaves do not dissolve well in water. For these mixtures, it would be necessary to use a different solvent. Your teacher may help you to carry out a chromatography experiment using one of these solvents, for example **propanone (acetone)**.

. . . .

Exercise 6.8

1. What is meant by the term 'chromatography'?

2. Give two examples where chromatography might be used to find out more about some mixtures.

3. What is a chromatogram?

4. Where would you find the most soluble dyes on a chromatogram?

5. If a dye did not move up the paper at all, what does this tell you about the dye?

6. Draw a neat, labelled diagram, showing how you would set up a chromatography experiment to compare the colours in the inks from three fountain pens.

7. Here is a picture of a chromatogram obtained by some children comparing some different green felt pen inks. Look at it carefully and then answer the questions.

    (a) How many different felt pens did the children use?

    (b) How many different yellow dyes are shown on the chromatogram? Explain your answer.

    (c) How many blue dyes are shown?

    (d) Which pen was made using just one dye?

    (e) Which two pens do you think might have been made by the same manufacturer? Explain your answer.

Chapter 7: Chemical changes

What is a chemical change?

In *Junior Science Book 2* we learnt about some of the changes that take place when materials are heated or cooled. We learnt that ice changes to liquid water when heated; we call this change melting. Water can be frozen again to make ice, so melting is a **reversible** change. We can change water from a solid to a liquid and back to a solid again as many times as we like. It is still water, even though it has a different name (ice) when it is a solid. Nothing new is made when this change takes place. We change only the state of the water. We also learnt about evaporation and condensation. These changes are also reversible.

Some changes of state are reversible

Sometimes though when we heat materials something different happens. The process of heating changes the material so that a new substance or material is formed.

Here are some everyday examples. If we put an egg into hot water or into a hot frying pan the egg changes. The translucent egg white becomes opaque and solid and the runny yolk becomes harder. We cannot change it back into the runny egg that came out of the shell.

Cooking is a non-reversible change

When we make a cake, we mix flour, sugar, butter and egg together and put the mixture into the oven. When it comes out, the mixture looks quite different. We cannot change the delicious cake back into the ingredients again. A **non-reversible** change has happened.

In these examples something new is made when the material is heated. We call this type of change a **chemical change** or **chemical reaction**. The new materials are called the **products** of the reaction.

Some chemical changes occur without having to heat the materials. The materials just need to be mixed together and they **react**. We will learn about this type of reaction later in the chapter.

Exercise 7.1

Are the following changes reversible or non-reversible?

1. Melting chocolate

2. Burning a candle

3. Baking bread

4. Freezing juice to make an ice lolly

5. Drying clothes

An important chemical change – combustion

Combustion is the scientific name for **burning**. You will often have seen things burning. Maybe your parents have a bonfire in the garden or candles on the table for dinner. Perhaps there is a lovely warm fire in your living room.

Sometimes things burn when we don't want them to. Fires in forests and woods can cause a lot of damage. Sometimes these fires reach people's homes and can kill people. Fire is dangerous, so it is important to treat it very carefully. You should never play around with fire as you could get hurt or cause a fire in your home, school or elsewhere.

Combustion is a dangerous non-reversible change

For combustion to take place three important things are needed. There has to be:

- a **fuel**, something that will burn (This could be a fossil fuel, such as coal, oil or gas but it could also be wood, paper or candle wax. Many materials make good fuels.)

- an air supply (or **oxygen**)

- a source of heat to start the reaction

These three things are often shown on a diagram called a **fire triangle**.

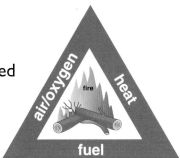

If one of these three factors is missing, combustion cannot occur. Fire fighters know this and so, when they put out a fire, they usually spray lots of water onto it. This removes the heat and also blocks the air from the fire. Some fires, however, cannot be put out using water. For example, you should never pour water onto a fire in a frying pan or chip fryer. The fire is very hot and the water would quickly turn to steam and make the burning fat spit out all over the place. This would make the fire worse. Can you explain why water should never be used on a fire in an electrical device?

Sometimes a **fire blanket** can be used to put out a fire. Can you explain how this would work? Have a look at the **fire extinguishers** around your school *but do not touch them*. You may be able to see a label telling you what they have in them. Some contain a **foam** and some contain **carbon dioxide**. Both of these put out fires by blocking the air supply.

To do: Make a fire extinguisher

You should wear eye protection to do this experiment and should not do it without an adult to help you.

You will need:

- plastic bag (with either a zip lock or wire tie)
- vinegar, 2 tablespoons
- bicarbonate of soda, 1 tablespoon
- candle securely held in a sand tray
- matches or a lighter
- safety goggles or glasses

1. Open your bag and put the bicarbonate of soda into the bag.

2. Pour the vinegar into the bag and then quickly seal the bag with the wire tie or the zip lock.

3. Watch what happens to the bag.

When the vinegar and the bicarbonate of soda come together a chemical reaction takes place. New products are formed. One of the products is a gas, carbon dioxide. Because the gas takes up more space than the materials you put into the bag, the bag inflates like a balloon.

Ask an adult to light the candle for you. Ask the adult to help you hold the bag near the candle but not directly over the flame. Position the bag so that the opening points towards the flame and open it carefully. Make sure it is not tipped so that any liquid comes out. The gas will pour out over the candle and put it out. Pure carbon dioxide is heavier than the mixture of gases that make up the air so it sinks down and surrounds the candle, stopping the air from reaching it.

Bicarbonate of soda is used in baking to make cakes rise. It reacts with other materials in the cake mix and makes bubbles of carbon dioxide. The bubbles get trapped in the cake mix and the cake rises.

Exercise 7.2

Use the words in the box to complete the following sentences. Each word may be used once, more than once or not at all.

> lighter   coal   fat   heat   heavier   air supply   water   gas   oil
> carbon dioxide   combustion   fuel   fire extinguisher   air   electrical

1. The scientific name for burning is _____ .

2. The three parts of the fire triangle are _____ , _____ and an _____ _____ .

3. The three types of fossil fuel are _____ , _____ and _____ .

4. A _____ _____ is a device used to put out a fire by blocking the _____ _____ .

5. Water should never be used to put out fires in _____ devices or burning _____ .

6. _____ _____ gas is used to put out fires because it is _____ than air.

· ·

More about candles

What really happens when a candle burns?

Have you ever wondered what happens when a candle burns? We all know that the candle gets smaller when it burns but why does this happen? Where does the candle wax go?

Let's see if we can work out what is happening.

To do: Investigate a burning candle

You should wear eye protection to do this experiment and should not do it without an adult to help you.

Getting smaller?

You will need:

- candle
- scales
- sand tray and/or a candle holder
- match or lighter
- safety goggles or glasses

1. Weigh the candle accurately and record its mass.

2. Fix the candle securely in a sand tray or candle holder. Put it in a place where it will not be knocked over or brushed against. Ask an adult to check that it is safe.

3. Then ask an adult to help you to light the candle safely and leave it to burn for about half an hour.

4. Blow out the candle very carefully. Make sure you do not blow away any melted wax from the candle. Leave it to cool.

5. Predict what you will find when you weigh the candle again. How heavy do you think it will be?

6. When the candle is cool and the wax has all solidified, weigh it again. Was your prediction correct?

When we burn a candle, a chemical reaction takes place. Remember the fire triangle. Where did heat to start the combustion reaction come from? What is the fuel?

Often people think that the wick is the fuel. The wick is usually made from cotton string. It actually does not burn very well but glows hot enough to melt and then evaporate the candle wax. It is the wax **vapour** that burns.

To do: Investigate a burning candle (continued)

The air supply

You will need:

- night light candle
- sand tray
- match or lighter
- jam jars of different sizes
- timer
- safety goggles or glasses

1. Place the candle safely in the sand tray.

2. Ask an adult to help you to light the candle safely.

3. Carefully place one of the jam jars upside down over the candle and push it down into the sand.

4. Watch what happens.

5. Try this again with the same jam jar and time how long the candle takes to go out.

6. Now try with the other jam jars. Predict how long you think it will take for each candle to go out. Can you see a pattern in the results?

When you put a cover over the candle like this, the candle eventually goes out. Why do you think this happens?

To do: Investigate a burning candle (continued)

The products of the reaction

You will need:

- candle

- sand tray and/or candle holder

- match or lighter

- large jam jar

- safety goggles or glasses

1. Place the candle carefully in the sand tray or candle holder and ask an adult to check that it is safe.

2. Then ask an adult to help you to light the candle safely.

3. Turn the jam jar over and place it over the candle as before and watch carefully.

You already know what will happen to the candle. This time look carefully at the sides of the jam jar. What can you see? Can you guess what this is?

Let us think about the results of these experiments. The candle gets lighter when it burns. It gets shorter too and we cannot bring the candle back to its original size. A non-reversible chemical reaction has taken place.

When you put jars of different sizes over the candle, the candle went out. The larger the jar, the longer the candle should have burnt before it went out. The candle needs something from the air to burn. About four-fifths of air is a gas called **nitrogen**. Most of the rest of the air is oxygen and this is what the candle needs. When the candle burned it used the oxygen in the jar. The candle went out when there was not enough oxygen left to keep it burning.

When the candle burned in the jar, did you see the jar becoming misty as water vapour condensed on the sides of the jar? Water vapour is one of the products of the combustion reaction. Another product created is the gas carbon dioxide. You may remember that you learnt in *Junior Science Book 2* that this gas is formed when fuels burn.

We can test whether a gas is carbon dioxide by using a liquid called **lime water**. This looks like ordinary, clear water but when it is mixed with carbon dioxide, a reaction occurs and a white chalky suspension is formed, making the lime water go cloudy. If a candle is put into a large jam jar, lit and allowed to burn for a while and then carefully extinguished, we can pour a little lime water into the bottom of the jar and shake it around a bit. The lime water goes cloudy because the carbon dioxide formed when the candle was burning has stayed in the jar.

Burning candle

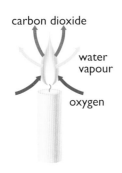

carbon dioxide

water vapour

oxygen

When a candle burns, the products are gases

When combustion takes place, the candle gets smaller because the particles making up the wax are used up when it burns, forming the gases carbon dioxide and water vapour. These gas products are then lost into the air. You may also have noticed some soot forming in the jam jar when you put it over the candle. Soot is formed during combustion if some of the fuel does not react fully with oxygen.

Lime water goes milky

Scientists often describe chemical reactions using something called a **word equation**. The word equation for combustion looks like this:

fuel + oxygen $\xrightarrow{\text{react to form}}$ water vapour + carbon dioxide

Exercise 7.3

1. Why does a candle go out if it is covered with a jar?

2. Name two gases that are found in the air.

3. Which gas makes up over three-quarters of the air?

4. Which gas in the air is needed for combustion?

5. What products are formed when a fuel such as candle wax burns in air?

Exercise 7.4: Extension question

Peter thinks that when a candle burns, all the wax melts and drips down the side. He says that the wax could be collected and made into a candle again, so combustion is a reversible change. What could you say and do to show Peter that he is wrong and that combustion is a non-reversible reaction?

Another chemical change – rusting

The car in this picture is very **rusty**. You must have seen other things go rusty too. How do you think things become rusty? Do all materials go rusty? Discuss your ideas with your partner or group.

Rusting is a chemical change

You have probably come up with several ideas. The children in this picture have also had some ideas. What do you think of their ideas?

I THINK THAT THERE IS RUST INSIDE THE NAIL. THE RAIN WASHES AWAY THE SURFACE AND EXPOSES THE RUST

I THINK THE RUST IS A LAYER OF MICROBES IN THE AIR WHICH SETTLE ON THE NAIL

I THINK THAT RUST IS MADE WHEN METALS AND WATER REACT TOGETHER

I THINK THAT IRON IN THE METAL REACTS WITH OXYGEN FROM THE AIR

To test your ideas you will need to do some experiments. First we will set up some experiments to find out whether it is water, air or both that make nails rust. You may be able to set up some extra experiments to test some of your ideas as well.

To do: What causes rusting

You will need:

- iron nails
- test tubes or other containers
- rubber bungs or lids to seal your containers
- boiled water
- oil
- silica gel
- labels

In order to find out which conditions are necessary for rusting, we need to set up situations where we can take away one condition at a time. By doing this we can see which conditions are needed for rust to appear and which are not. We need to keep all the other conditions the same to make our tests fair. If the nail does not rust then the condition we took away is needed for rusting to occur.

1. First set up your control experiment. Put a nail in a clean, dry container with no lid. Leave this out in the room during the experiment. You can check whether it has rusted and use it to compare with your other results. Label the container CONTROL.

2. Now set up the other conditions:

   (a) **Nail in contact with water and air**
   Place the nail in a container with a little water or maybe with some wet cotton wool or tissue. Put a lid on the container to keep the moisture in. There will be plenty of air trapped in the container. Label the container WATER AND AIR.

   (b) **Nail in contact with water but no air**
   Water contains dissolved air so the water must be boiled for a few minutes to remove the dissolved air. Your teacher will do this for you. Place your nail in the container and cover it with the boiled water. You can then float a layer of oil on the surface to act as a seal to keep the air out and stop any more air from dissolving in the water again. Label the container WATER, NO AIR.

(c) **Nail in contact with air but no water**
You need to seal the nail in a completely dry container. There is water vapour in the air so this needs to be removed. We can do this by putting a substance that absorbs water, **silica gel**, inside the dry container. It will absorb the water vapour and dry the air. You then need to seal the container tightly to make sure that no water vapour from the outside air gets in. Label the container AIR, NO WATER.

3. Set up any other experiments that you and your class want to try. Remember to label the containers to show what conditions the nails are in.

4. Place all your containers together somewhere where they can be left for a few days.

5. Which nails do you think will rust? Write down your predictions so you can remember them when you look at the results in a few days' time.

Your experiments should have shown that air and water together cause objects containing iron to rust. The damp iron reacts with oxygen from the air and makes a new substance. Did you find out anything else interesting about rusting in your experiments?

Iron is the only metal that rusts. Many objects you see becoming rusty are made from steel. **Steel** is a mixture of substances, including iron and carbon. It is the iron in steel that rusts. Other metals do react with oxygen but they do not form the reddish brown material we call rust. Silver tarnishes to make a dull grey coating. When copper is left in the air, it often forms a green substance called verdigris. Some metals react so quickly with oxygen that they burst into flames! We have to be very careful to store these so that no air can get to them.

Copper turns green when it reacts with the air

Does rusting use up air?

We have shown that rusting takes place when iron or steel comes into contact with air and water. We suggested that the iron reacted with the oxygen from the air. We can do an experiment to show that rusting uses up air.

To do: Using up air

You will need:

- iron wool
- large test tube (boiling tube)
- bowl of water
- retort stand and clamp or other way of supporting the test tube to stop it falling over

1. Take some of the iron wool and push it to the bottom of the test tube. Do not pack it too tightly. Check it will not fall out when the test tube is turned upside down.

2. Put some water in the test tube and shake it about a bit to make sure that the iron wool is really wet. Tip out the remaining water.

3. Turn the test tube upside down and put the opening just into the water in the bowl. You need to make sure that the opening of the test tube is under the surface of the water but do not push it too far down or you will not be able to see the results.

4. Clamp the tube firmly and put it somewhere where it will not be knocked or touched for about a week.

5. Take a look at your experiment each day. Can you explain what happens?

6. When there is no further change taking place, use a waterproof pen to mark the level of the water in the test tube. How much air has the rusting iron wool used up?

When the iron wool rusts, it uses up air, just like the candle did when it burned. As the air is used up, water is drawn up into the test tube to take the place of the used air. The water level rises but when about one-fifth of the air has been used up, the level stops rising. Why is this?

You may remember that we suggested that the iron uses oxygen when it rusts. When all the oxygen has been used up, no more rusting can occur. The experiment shows that oxygen makes up about one-fifth of the air.

Preventing rusting

Generally, rusting is rather a nuisance. When iron or steel rusts, a strong metal structure can change to crumbly brown rust. Objects can be spoilt by rust but there are ways to stop it.

Since rusting is caused by a combination of water and oxygen coming into contact with the iron, the best way to prevent it is to make sure that water and oxygen are kept away from the surface of the object. There are lots of ways of doing this. For example, the surface can be covered in oil or paint. See how many other different ways you and your partner or group can think of to keep oxygen and water away from the iron. Perhaps you could do some experiments to try out some of your ideas.

Many structures are protected from rusting by paint

Another way of keeping iron or steel objects from rusting is to cover them with a very thin layer of another metal that does not rust. This process is called **galvanisation** and the metal that is used is usually **zinc**.

First, the object is cleaned thoroughly, often by dipping it into a tank of acid. This removes dirt and any traces of rust from the surface of the object. It is then dipped into a tank of melted zinc. When it is taken out, the zinc sticks to the surface in a very thin layer. If you look closely at a galvanised surface,

Look closely at the surface of a galvanised object, such as a watering can, to see the zinc crystals on the surface

you can see beautiful crystals of zinc. This layer will stop the water and oxygen from reaching the surface of the iron or steel.

Did you know?
When we buy soup or tomatoes from the supermarket, they may be stored in metal cans. People often call these tins because the early cans were made from 'tinplate steel'. This steel is coated with a very thin layer of a metal called **tin** to prevent rusting. Nowadays the so-called 'tin cans' often have no tin in them at all. Although some steel cans are still galvanised with tin on the inside, some have a plastic coating and some are made from **aluminium**, which doesn't rust.

Exercise 7.5

1. What conditions cause iron to rust?

2. How can dissolved air be removed from water?

3. When you have removed the air from some water, how can you stop more air dissolving in the water?

4. Name a substance that can be used to absorb water vapour from the air.

5. Explain why steel objects rust.

6. If a car rusts a lot, it must be treated and mended before its owner is allowed to drive it again. Explain why rusting might make a car unsafe.

7. Bicycle frames are usually made from steel and they are painted to prevent rusting. The chain of the bicycle is also steel but it is not painted.
   (a) Why would painting the chain not be the best way to prevent rusting?
   (b) Suggest how the chain could be kept rust free.

8. (a) What is meant by the term 'galvanisation'?
   (b) Explain in your own words how an object is galvanised.

Exercise 7.6: Extension question

A sculptor makes a beautiful sculpture using steel. He likes the look of the shiny steel but he knows that it will soon rust when he puts it outside.

Write a letter to the sculptor, suggesting some ways in which he might be able to keep the sculpture looking shiny and new and describing how he could carry out a series of experiments to test some different methods to see how well they work.

Sometimes artists want their work to rust; the rusty red colour of this fox sculpture makes it look almost real

Chapter 8: Soils

What is soil?

We know that plants grow in **soil**. Soil is usually brown and may be crumbly or sticky. It is found almost everywhere but have you ever noticed that soils in different places, even quite close together, can be very different in colour and **texture**?

Let's start by taking a closer look at different types of soil.

Soil is needed to grow crops and other plants

To do: Compare soils

You will need:

- 3 soil samples
- 3 sheets of newspaper

Your teacher will provide you with some soil samples. Have a good look at them. Describe the smell and the colour. Feel the texture of the samples. What is the soil made of? What can it be used for? See if you can explain exactly what soil is. Note down your ideas and observations and discuss your findings.

Wash your hands when you have finished.

Soil A

Soil B

Soil C

Different soils may have very different properties

A rocky start

Soil covers a large proportion of the land and comes in many different colours and textures. If you rub soil between your fingers you should be able to feel gritty particles. These are tiny fragments of rock. Depending upon the type of rock or the mixture of rocks in your sample, soils can feel very different. In *Junior Science Book 1* we learnt that rocks can be sorted into three groups: sedimentary, igneous and metamorphic, depending on how they were formed.

There are many different rocks in each one of these groups because each rock is made from a different combination of **minerals**. Think about a visit to a baker's shop. You will see lots of different cakes with different colours and different textures; some with raisins, some with cherries, some with nuts or chocolate. They look different because they have been made with different ingredients, but they are all cakes. So it is with rocks. Some rocks are made of just one mineral; others are made from two or more minerals. The colour and texture of the rock will depend on the minerals that are in it. For example, granite (an igneous rock) is made from a combination of the minerals **quartz**, **mica** and **feldspar**. If you look closely at a piece of granite with a lens, you may be able to see white areas which are quartz, black areas which are mica and pinkish areas which are feldspar. The colour, texture and chemistry of the soil on the surface is affected by the type of rock beneath the surface.

Did you know?
Archaeologists can identify the birthplace of ancient human remains found during excavations by investigating the minerals in their teeth. The minerals in the soil of each region will be slightly different because of the different rocks in the area. These minerals are taken up by plants, and then absorbed into the bodies of people who eat the plants. Our teeth are not likely to be as interesting to future archaeologists because we now eat foods from all around the world.

From rock to soil

But how does a rocky mountain become a piece of grit in the soil in our flowerbed? Although rocks seem strong and hard, they can be gradually broken down by the weather. Rain, wind and changes in temperature have a large part to play in this process. Water collects in the cracks and crevices in the rocks on a mountain side and then freezes when it is cold. Water expands when it freezes and takes up more space and so the pieces of rock are forced apart and lumps of rock are broken off. The broken pieces of rock may bounce down the mountainside, being chipped into smaller pieces as they go. Pieces of rock may land in a stream and, as the water gathers speed, they may be dragged along, rubbing against boulders at the side of the river and splitting into smaller and smaller pieces. These tiny crumbs of rock may settle at the sides of a river or at the mouth of a river where it flows into the sea.

Rocks in moving streams and rivers are broken into smaller pieces

Rain water is also responsible for dissolving some of the minerals in rocks, making cracks and crevices so that more water can get in and freeze, forcing the lumps of rock apart. The landscape of mountains and rocks is always changing and this process is called **weathering**. Some of the rock pieces will finish up in the sea but many will remain on land and become part of the soil.

To do: The power of ice

You will need:

- small plastic drinks bottle
- water
- foil

1. Fill your bottle to the top with water.

2. Then place a piece of tin foil over the top to make a lid.

3. Place your bottle, the right way up, in a freezer and leave it until the water freezes. After two days, remove the bottle from the freezer.

The water in your bottle will have turned into ice and because the ice takes up more space than water it will have pushed off the foil lid. Why do you think you used a plastic bottle instead of a glass bottle? If you had used a glass bottle, what might have happened when the water froze?

Exercise 8.1

Use the words in the box to fill in the gaps in the sentences below. Each word may be used once, more than once or not at all.

> colour   minerals   weathering   texture   rain   temperature
> wind   gritty   granite   soil

1. Rocks are made from lots of different _____ .

2. The different minerals in rocks will give the rock its _____ and _____ .

3. Rocks are broken into smaller pieces by _____ , _____ and changes in _____ .

4. The process in which rocks are broken down into tiny pieces is called _____ .

5. Tiny crumbs of rock give the soil a _____ texture.

Exercise 8.2

1. Explain how water can make rocks crack apart when it freezes.

2. Draw a series of pictures showing the weathering process, showing how a large boulder on a mountain is broken up, and becomes smaller and smaller on its journey down the mountain towards the sea.

Something else is needed

These tiny particles of rock are not the whole story. They need to combine with something else if they are to become the nutritious soil in a flowerbed.

Decomposers such as fungi break down dead plant material to form humus

Plants need to take in small quantities of nutrients from the soil in order to stay healthy. The nutrients in the soil come from all the dead and decaying plant and animal remains that lie on the ground. Leaves fall from the trees in autumn. Flowers, which are so beautiful in summer, die back and fall to the ground. Dead branches and rotting fruit fall from trees. The fox leaves scraps of food on the ground after eating a rabbit and the owl drops pellets on the ground after eating a mouse. Half-eaten acorns are left by the squirrel and seeds drop in bird droppings. All these things and many more lie on the ground, decompose and combine with the gritty rock particles to become the soil that is so essential for life on Earth. These dead plant and animal remains in the soil are called **humus**, and are the sticky particles in the soil.

Humus is an important source of nutrients for plants. It also helps to hold water in the soil and stops it drying out and being washed or blown away. Water is absorbed by the plants through their roots. The film of water that forms around the small crumbs of soil also provides a habitat for tiny **micro-organisms**.

Air is also a very important ingredient in the composition of soil. Air spaces in between the crumbs of soil provide oxygen for all the organisms that live in the soil, including the roots of plants.

A good sample of soil will have plenty of humus combined with gritty particles of rock, with plenty of gaps for air and water.

Getting the right mixture

Some soils have a sticky texture and some have a more gritty texture. Rub different soil samples between your fingers, can you feel the difference? The soil with a sticky texture will probably have more **clay** particles in the mixture. Clay particles are very small, with tiny air spaces in between. The water gathers in the tiny spaces and is held there and tends to keep the soil heavy and damp. This type of soil does not make such a good habitat for micro-organisms. Can you explain why? Gardeners will sometimes try to increase the air spaces in clay soil by digging in **grit**.

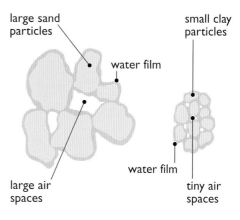

large sand particles

water film

large air spaces

small clay particles

water film

tiny air spaces

Larger particles have bigger air spaces between them

The structure of the soil changes as you dig down deeper and deeper

If the particles are a little larger than the clay particles, they are called **sand**. Soil with a sandy texture has more air spaces, which allows the water to drain through more easily, and provides channels where the roots of plants can grow.

We can improve the fertility of the soil by increasing the amount of humus. Garden waste and vegetable peelings are an excellent source of extra humus in the soil. We can put them in a **compost** heap to be broken down by decomposers. This creates a crumbly mixture that can be added to the soil.

Kitchen and garden waste can be turned into humus in a compost bin

A soil that has the right mixture of sand, clay and humus will have good drainage but will also hold enough water for plants to grow. It will be **fertile**, which means it has plenty of nutrients in it. This type of soil is called **loam**. Farmers and gardeners try to improve their soil to make a loam so their plants will grow well.

Did you know?
One gram of soil may contain a billion micro-organisms, which may be of over a million different types.

Exercise 8.3

1. Give at least three examples of things that were once living that may become part of the soil.

2. What name is given to the material in the soil that is made from the remains of dead animals and plants?

3. Why is this material important in the soil?

4. Why is it important to have air spaces in the soil?

5. What is the difference between the particles in clay and the particles in sand?

6. Which soil will allow water to drain through more quickly: a clay soil or a sandy soil?

7. What is meant by the term 'fertile'?

8. What is loam?

9. Why do gardeners and farmers like loamy soil to grow their plants in?

10. How does a compost heap help gardeners to improve their soil?

Finding out more about soils

There are several ways of finding out more about the type of soil you have in your garden. The first thing to do is to find out about the different particle sizes in your soil. There are two ways to do this.

To do: Soil soup

You will need:

- jar with a screw top lid

- soil sample

- water

1. Half fill your jar with soil.

2. Pour in some water until your jar is nearly full. Screw on the lid securely.

3. Now give your jar a thorough shake. Find a safe place to leave your soil soup and leave it for 24 hours.

When you next look at your soil soup you should be able to see that your sample has settled into different layers.

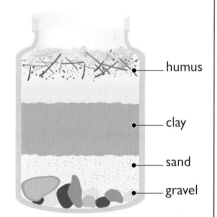

Now draw a diagram to show your soil soup and label the different layers. Notice how the **gravel** (larger stones) has settled at the bottom, the more gritty sandy grains on top of the gravel and the finer clay particles above that. The leafy, twiggy pieces of humus should be floating on the surface of the water. Look at the colour of the water. Do you think anything from the soil has dissolved in the water?

If other members of your class have made soil soup with different types of soil, compare them carefully. What differences can you see between the samples?

To do: Soil sieves

Another way of separating the different ingredients in your soil is to use a set of sieves, each with holes of a slightly different size.

You will need:

- 500 g dry soil
- set of soil sieves
- sheets of newspaper (one for each sieve)
- scales

1. First of all, take a careful look at your set of sieves and notice the difference between the sizes of the holes in each sieve.

2. Put the sieves in order with the one with the largest holes at the top, and the sieve with the smallest holes at the bottom. You are going to put your soil sample into the top sieve, the one with the largest holes. Can you predict what is going to happen to your soil when you shake the apparatus?

3. Now place your sample of soil into the top layer of your set of sieves and put the lid on.

4. Carefully shake the sieves.

5. When you have given your soil a good shake, carefully remove the lid, and gently separate the sieves, placing each sieve on to a separate sheet of newspaper.

6. Carefully tip the contents of each sieve onto the sheet of newspaper. What do you notice about the particle size in each layer of the apparatus?

7. Fold the paper so that you can collect your sample and weigh each layer of soil.

8. Arrange your samples in order, from the coarsest to the finest particles and record the mass of each sample. You could draw a bar chart to show your results.

Can you explain why it was important to have a dry sample of soil?

You could now try this experiment with another soil sample and compare the results. What differences are there? Which soil sample do you think would be best for growing seeds?

The size of the particles in your soil affect how quickly water can drain through it. If water drains too quickly, the soil dries out quickly and there will be no water for the roots of plants to absorb. If water drains too slowly, it fills up all the air spaces in the soil and the roots of the plants and the other organisms in the soil will die from lack of oxygen. A good loamy soil is somewhere between the two.

To do: Test the drainage

In this experiment you are going to carry out a fair test to find out which of your soil samples lets water drain through fastest. Start by looking at your samples and feeling them. Maybe you have already found out about the particle sizes in your soils. Use this information to predict which soil you think will drain quickest.

You will need:

- small pieces of disposable cloth (one for each soil sample)
- funnel
- large measuring cylinder
- dry soil samples
- water
- beaker
- stop clock or watch

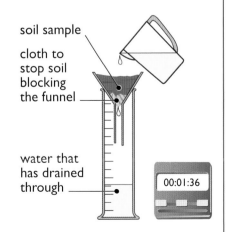

soil sample

cloth to stop soil blocking the funnel

water that has drained through

00:01:36

1. Place a small piece of cloth into the funnel to cover the hole at the bottom. This will stop your soil falling through and blocking the funnel.

2. Sit the funnel in the measuring cylinder so that you can easily measure the volume of water that drains through the soil.

3. Pour one dry soil sample into the funnel. To make it a fair test, you need to use the same depth of soil for each test, so mark the level you use for the first sample.

4. Put some water in a beaker. Start the stop clock and pour the water steadily onto the soil sample in your funnel, so that the water is always kept 'topped up'. After one minute, stop pouring and quickly measure how much water has passed through the soil into the measuring cylinder. Record the result carefully.

5. Empty the measuring cylinder, clean out the funnel, put a fresh piece of cloth in the bottom and repeat the test using another soil sample.

6. When you have tested all your samples, compare the results. Which soil drained quickest? Was your prediction correct?

These experiments should have taught you a lot about different soil samples. There are other tests that gardeners and farmers carry out to find out about the chemistry of their soils. You may have helped your parents to carry out some of these at home. You may do these yourself at school later when you know a little more about the chemistry involved.

Exercise 8.4

1. Some children were comparing soil samples. They placed some of each soil in a jar, added water and shook them. After two days the samples looked like this.

    (a) Which sample has more gravel in it?

    (b) Which sample contains less clay?

    (c) Which sample do you think might be described as loam? Explain your answer.

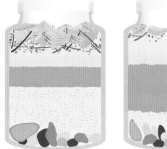

1.   2.

2. The table below shows the results obtained when two soil samples were separated using soil sieves.

Sieve layer	Mass in each layer, in grams	
	Soil A	Soil B
Top (largest holes)	80	50
Middle	40	20
Lower (smallest holes)	10	40
Bottom tray	20	
Total mass of sample		150

(a) Calculate the total mass of the sample of soil A.

(b) Calculate the mass found in the bottom tray for soil B

(c) Which sample might be described as a clay soil? Explain your answer.

(d) Which sample do you think would allow water to pass through more easily? Explain your answer.

(e) Draw a bar chart to show both sets of results. You will need to draw two bars for each sieve layer, one for each soil sample.

3. Mr Barleycorn wants to find out which of his fields would be best to grow a new crop. He has been told that the plants like a really well-drained soil. He needs to know which of his soils allows the water to drain through fastest.

(a) What advice would you give him about what to look for when he first examines his soils?

(b) Describe clearly how he could carry out an experiment to compare the drainage rates of his soils. Remember to say how he would tell which soil has the best drainage.

Life in the soil

There is another important part of the soil we have not looked at yet: the living things found in soil. There will be millions of tiny micro-organisms that we cannot see unless we use a microscope. There may be small invertebrates we would not normally notice and there can also be larger animals, such as worms or moles.

To do: Find life in the soil

You will need:

- plastic sieve or colander with holes about 0.5 cm in diameter
- bowl, preferably a white one, and deep enough so the sieve/colander does not touch the bottom
- sample of fresh damp soil
- lamp
- tray or container to put the animals in while you are looking at them
- hand lens

1. Place the sieve or colander in the bowl. Put your soil sample in the sieve or colander and position the lamp above the soil, but not touching it. Switch on the lamp and leave it on for about one and a half hours.

   Small animals in the soil prefer the cool damp conditions underground. When they feel soil becoming warmer, they move deeper into the soil. This helps to stop them becoming **dehydrated** on hot sunny days. It will also happen in your experiment; any small animals in the soil will move away from the warmth of the lamp and will fall through the holes in the sieve or colander and into the bowl below.

2. Turn off the lamp and carefully remove the sieve or colander. Gently collect any animals that you find in the bowl. Tip them onto the tray so you can study them closely with a hand lens. How many different types of animal have you collected?

Remember to return all animals to their soil and replace the soil sample where you found it.

Wash your hands when you have finished handling the soil.

The earthworm

Earthworms perform a very important role in the soil by mixing everything together. Earthworms burrow and wriggle in the soil and create channels through the soil for water, roots and air spaces. They pull dead and decaying material from the surface deep into the soil. This increases the amount of humus in the soil. There are lots of different types of earthworm. If you dig up a sample of soil in your garden, you may be surprised at how many different types of worm you can find. You may be able to find a key on the internet to help you identify them.

We can see the way that earthworms change the soil by collecting some and placing them in a wormery.

To do: Observe life in a wormery

You will need:

- wormery or large jam jar

- several soil samples

- sand

- leaves

- water

- a few large worms

- black card or cloth (large enough to cover the wormery or jam jar)

To do: Observe life in a wormery (continued)

1. Place layers of soil in your wormery with a thin layer of sand in between each layer.

2. Place a few leaves on the surface and pour in enough water to moisten the soil but not to flood it.

3. Place your worms carefully on the surface.

4. Cover the wormery with black card or a dark cloth and put it in a cool place.

5. After a few days remove the dark cover, and you should be able to see the tunnels in the soil where the worms have been moving up and down in the soil. Gradually the layers in the soil will become mixed as the worms burrow up and down. Make sure that the soil in your wormery does not dry out. When you have finished, return your worms to the place where you found them.

Did you know?
Some people believe that if you chop an earthworm in half, you will get two earthworms. This is not true. The cut end of one part of the unfortunate worm may heal and the worm may survive but you are most likely to finish up with two halves of a dead earthworm!

Exercise 8.5

Use the words in the box to fill in the gaps in the sentences below. Each word may be used once, more than once or not at all.

> roots   humus   micro-organisms   air   earthworms   water
> leaves   moles   invertebrates   sand

1. Soil contains millions of _____ which we cannot see without a microscope.

2. Some small _____ spend their lives in the soil.

3. Larger animals in the soil may include _____ and _____ .

4. Earthworms are useful in the soil because their burrows let _____ and _____ into the soil and make space for _____ to grow.

5. Earthworms also pull _____ into their burrows, which increases the amount of _____ in the soil.

· ·

Exercise 8.6: Extension questions

Read the following information about worms.

Earthworms spend most of their lives underground in the soil where it is cool and damp. They have to keep their skin moist because they breathe by absorbing oxygen through their skin. They come to the surface, usually at night, to collect leaves and pull them down into their burrows to eat. They will normally only come out during the day if it is raining and their burrows become flooded.

As they tunnel through the soil they take it into their mouths. The soil passes through their gut and some of the humus in the soil is digested. The remaining soil is passed out and makes a little squiggly mound called a wormcast. The worms make their wormcasts at the top of their burrows on the surface.

Earthworms are eaten by many animals, such as birds, hedgehogs and badgers. They have little bristles on the sides of their bodies, which they can use to anchor themselves into their burrows when they are attacked. This makes it difficult for predators to pull them out.

1. Biologists have observed that worms tend to move upwards through the soil in wet weather and downwards in hot weather. Suggest why they behave in this way.

2. Suggest how you might be able to estimate the number of worms under your lawn without digging them all up.

3. Write a story about a day in the life of an earthworm. Try to make your story exciting.

Chapter 9: Hear the sound

Sounds are made when something vibrates

Take a moment and listen carefully. What can you hear? You might be able to hear a bell ringing, people shouting, a bird singing or a bee buzzing.

The sounds you hear are created by something **vibrating**. When something vibrates it moves backwards and forwards very quickly and makes the air around it vibrate as well. The sound is carried to your ears by the vibrating air. Sometimes you can see vibrations. For example, if you stretch an elastic band on your fingers and pluck it you will see the band vibrating backwards and forwards.

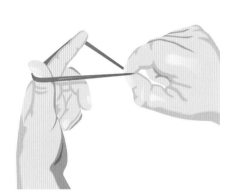

To do: A vibrating ruler

You will need:

- ruler
- table

Place the ruler on the edge of the table so that about half of it is sticking out. Place your hand firmly over the end of the ruler on the table and gently flick the other end. Do not flick it too hard or it might snap.

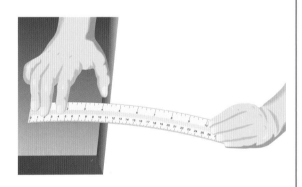

You should be able to see the ruler moving up and down. What sound can you hear? The air around the ruler is being made to vibrate and these vibrations carry the sound to your ear.

Now move the ruler and change the **length** of the piece overhanging the table. Flick your ruler gently again and observe the difference in the vibrations. Think about the change in the sound it makes.

If you have a metre ruler, predict what will happen if you carry out the test again using this longer ruler. Will the vibrations be larger or smaller? What sort of sound will be made? Now try it. Were your predictions correct?

Vibrations are not always visible

There are many occasions when you may be able to hear a sound but not be able to see the vibrations. For example, when you blow a recorder you will hear the sound but you will not be able to see the recorder vibrating.

To do: See vibrations

You will need:

- drum or jam jar with a lid of stretched clingfilm held on with an elastic band
- salt
- drumstick or pencil
- tuning fork
- shallow dish of water

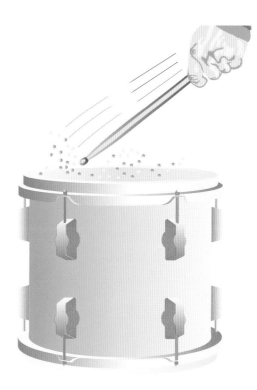

1. Sprinkle a layer of salt on the surface of the drum and tap it with your drumstick. The grains of salt jump around as the skin on the drum vibrates. We know that the drum skin is vibrating, even though we may not be able to see the drum skin moving, because we can see the salt jumping.

2. Strike the tuning fork gently on the edge of the table. Look at it carefully. You may be able to see the prongs vibrating. Put the tip of the vibrating tuning fork into the dish of water. The vibrations of the tuning fork make the water move and splash about.

Hearing sounds

Sounds create vibrations, so when we hear a sound it is because our ears are feeling the vibrations in the air. The vibrating air enters our ears and makes our **eardrums** vibrate. The eardrum is a tiny layer of skin inside our ear that moves backwards and forwards as the vibrating air hits it. The vibrating eardrum causes three little bones in the middle part of our ear to vibrate too. These vibrations are then carried into the inner part of the ear where the nerves change the vibrations into electrical signals that are sent to the brain.

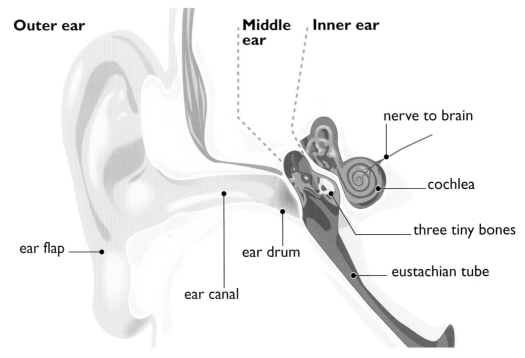

Outer ear   **Middle ear**   **Inner ear**

nerve to brain

cochlea

three tiny bones

ear flap

ear drum

eustachian tube

ear canal

The visible, outer part of the ear channels sounds into the ear. Some animals can move their ears around slightly so that they can collect sounds more efficiently. Different animals have ears of different sizes and shapes. Do you think this makes a difference to the way they hear?

To do: Large or small ears?

Work with a partner to experiment and find out whether larger or smaller ears help you to hear more easily. Remember never make very **loud** or sudden noises close to someone's ear because it can cause damage to the eardrum.

Cup your hands around your ears to extend your outer ears. Ask your partner to stand in different places in the room and make various sounds, some **soft** and some louder. Each time your partner makes a noise, listen with your hands cupped around your ears and then take your hands away from your ears. What differences do you notice?

Does the way that you hold your hands to your ears make a difference to how well you can hear?

Before hearing aids were invented people who were hard of hearing used ear trumpets to help them to hear

Try making huge 'elephant ears' from card and use them to see if they make a difference to how well you can hear.

Having two ears helps you to work out where the sound is coming from. Each ear receives the vibrations but the ear closer to the source of the sound will hear it a little more loudly and slightly before the other.

Can you think of another sense we have where receiving information from two sources makes the information much more accurate?

Predators, such as foxes, need good hearing to help them locate their prey

A fox hunting for food at night will use its senses of sight and smell and its hearing. For example, a fox may sniff and peer into some thick grass, and move its head from side to side. As it does this, each ear may receive the vibrations made by a mouse, allowing the fox to pinpoint exactly where it is.

To do: Find the sound source

You will need:

- 2 pieces of plastic tubing each about 60 cm in length
- 2 plastic funnels
- sticky tape
- ruler or piece of wood about 30 cm in length

1. Place a funnel into each piece of tubing and fix with sticky tape. Then hold the funnels onto the ruler so that they face in opposite directions, and fix with tape.

2. Cross the two pieces of tubing over and hold one end to each ear. Try to make a good seal with your hands to prevent too many other noises getting in.

3. Close your eyes and ask your partner to stand on one side of you and clap their hands or make a noise. Can you tell where your partner is standing?

Because you have crossed the tubing, the sound made on one side of you is heard by the ear on the other side. Your brain may be confused and think the source of the sound is on the opposite side to where it really came from.

Exercise 9.1

Use the words in the box to fill in the gaps in the sentences below. Each word may be used once, more than once or not at all.

> sound   two   vibrations   cannot   backwards   see   can
> forwards   three   eardrum   ears   five   canal

1. Sounds create _____ in the air.

2. When something vibrates it moves _____ and _____ very quickly.

3. The vibrating air carries the sound to your _____ .

4. When an elastic band is plucked you can _____ the band vibrating.

5. When a recorder is played, vibrations are made even though you _____ see them.

6. The vibrating air travels into the ear and makes the _____ vibrate.

7. There are _____ little bones in our ears that vibrate.

8. We have _____ ears, which helps us to work out exactly where the _____ is coming from.

. . . .

Exercise 9.2

1. Describe in your own words how you hear the sound made when the school bell rings.

2. What is the function of the outer part of your ear?

3. What difficulties might you have if you only had one ear rather than two?

4. How does a fox use its hearing to pinpoint the exact position of a prey animal it cannot see?

Exercise 9.3: Extension question

Most of us rely on our hearing for many different activities during the day. Deaf people are unable to make use of sound to help them sense their environment. Make a list of some activities where hearing people rely on sound and state what can be done to make these activities possible for deaf people.

To do: Ear bones

Find out the names given to the three little bones in the middle part of your ear. One of the bones is the smallest bone in your body. What is it called?

Did you know?
Your ears also help you to **balance**. There are small canals in the inner part of your ears, which are full of liquid. As you move around, the liquid pushes past tiny hairs in the canals. The movement of the hairs creates messages which are sent to the brain. The reason you feel dizzy after spinning around in circles is because the liquid in the canals keeps moving after you have stopped spinning. So the information received by the brain from the eyes and canals in the ear is confusing!

Sounds travel

Vibrations not only travel through air to our ears but they can also travel through other materials. Place your ear on a table and gently tap on the underside of the table. Listen carefully. Now tap closer to your ear and then further away. Continue tapping gently and lift your head from the table. Did you hear the sound more clearly when your ear was on the table or above it? Was the sound louder when your tapping was nearer or further away from your ear?

Sound travels best when travelling through hard materials. Vibrations can travel a long way through the ground or hard material like steel. They travel about 15 times faster through steel than when they travel through air.

Did you know?
A bird searching for its food will detect a worm by feeling the vibrations of the worm scraping through the soil under the surface. The bird feels the vibrations through its feet as well as hearing the sounds of the moving prey with their ears.

A snake will sense danger by feeling the vibrations of footsteps on the ground.

A fish will feel sound vibrations in the water through its body.

Many birds can detect their prey underground or hidden under the bark of a tree

The aye-aye uses its long finger like a drumstick

Did you know?

The aye-aye of Madagascar has a very long middle finger on each of its front feet. It uses this finger like a drumstick. It taps on the bark of a tree and the vibrations it feels help it to discover if there are insect larvae hidden underneath. If there are, it then uses its strong incisor teeth to bite through the wood to reach the food. Aye-ayes also eat coconuts and will often tap on a coconut to find out how much liquid is inside before choosing which one to gnaw.

To do: Can you hear me?

You will need:

- 2 paper or plastic cups
- piece of string 4 or 5 metres long

1. Make a neat hole in the bottom of each cup and thread the string through the hole. Make a knot at the end of the string inside each cup.

2. Ask your partner to hold one cup while you hold the other. Move apart until the string is pulled tight. Hold your cup to your ear and ask your partner to speak quietly into their cup. Can you hear what is being said?

3. Now change over and let your partner listen to you speaking.

4. Experiment with the **tightness** of the string. Is it easier to hear your partner if the string is tight or is it easier to hear if the string is loose?

5. You could try again using a different thickness of string to see if this makes any difference. Or you could try with a different length of string, or a different sized cup. What will you need to do to make the test fair?

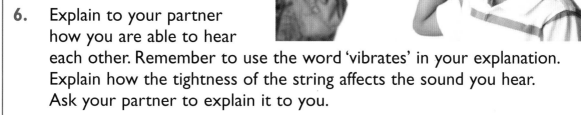

6. Explain to your partner how you are able to hear each other. Remember to use the word 'vibrates' in your explanation. Explain how the tightness of the string affects the sound you hear. Ask your partner to explain it to you.

7. Write down a really good explanation by sharing your ideas and then make a presentation to your class.

Sound vibrations travel through air and solids but do you think they can travel through liquids?

When you swim underwater you can still hear the sounds of people at the edge of the pool. The water changes the vibrations and they do not travel in quite the same way as they do through air. The voices that you hear through water sound different than when you hear them through air. Sound travels about four times faster through water than it does through air.

Here on Earth there are almost always sounds around us: the noise of traffic, the sound of voices, the rustling of leaves or wind in the grass. It is very difficult to find a place that is without noise.

Vibrations from sounds need to have something to travel through if we are to hear them. We have learnt how sound can travel through solids, liquids and gases. A place that is completely empty, where there are no solids, liquids or gases is called a **vacuum**. In a vacuum it is completely silent because there is nothing to carry the vibrations.

On Earth, there is air all around us so it is difficult to create a vacuum. In space, however, it is very different. In space there is no air to carry the vibrations and therefore it is always silent.

You cannot be heard in the vacuum of space because sounds need a medium to travel through

In a thunderstorm the light reaches our eyes some time before the sound reaches our ears

Did you know?
The crash of thunder and the flash of lightning happen at the same time. However, light travels faster to our eyes than the sound vibrations travel to our ears, so we see the flash before we hear the crash. The further away the thunderstorm, a longer time will pass between the flash and the crash.

To do: Seeing and hearing

You will need:

● 2 cymbals

Your teacher will ask one person to take the cymbals and walk away from the rest of the class across the playing field. They should then turn to face the class. Your teacher will give a signal and the person with the cymbals will bang the

cymbals together. Watch and listen carefully. Do you see the action or hear the sound first? Carry out the action again, and watch and listen carefully.

Exercise 9.4

Use the words in the box to fill in the gaps in the sentences below. Each word may be used once, more than once or not at all.

> noisy   see   hard   silent   solids   light   gases   four   hear
> fifteen   vacuum   liquids   sound   ten   soft

1. Sound vibrations can travel through _____ , _____ and _____ but not through a _____ .

2. Sound travels best through _____ materials.

3. Sound travels about _____ times faster when travelling through hard materials than through air.

4. Sounds in water travel _____ times faster than sounds in the air.

5. In space it is _____ .

6. In a thunderstorm we _____ the lightning before we _____ the thunder because _____ travels faster than _____ .

Music to my ears

All musical instruments create their sounds by making something vibrate.

- Playing a note on a piano causes a hammer to hit the strings making them vibrate.

- Violin strings are made to vibrate by plucking them with a finger or moving a bow across them.

- Cymbals crash together pushing away the air between them, causing vibrations.

- A clarinet has a thin piece of wood in the mouthpiece, called a reed. When you blow through the mouthpiece the reed vibrates and makes the **column** of air inside the clarinet vibrate.

Each instrument in the orchestra makes vibrations in different ways

- A trumpet player makes his lips vibrate when he blows into the trumpet making the column of air inside the trumpet vibrate.

- When you speak or sing, the air from your lungs moves over the vocal cords in your throat and makes them vibrate.

Place your hand on your throat and make singing and speaking sounds. Can you feel the vibrations?

Changing pitch

Musical instruments can usually make more than one sound. The sound might be high or low, loud or soft. The changes in the vibrations make these different sounds. Place your hand on your throat again, and sing 'la' in a low voice. Can you feel the vibrations? Now sing again in a high voice and feel your throat again. The vibrations made in your throat this time should feel much faster and make your hand buzz.

Think back to the beginning of the chapter and try the test with your ruler again. Let most of the ruler stick out over the edge of the desk and as you flick the ruler, listen to the sound and observe the speed of the vibrations.

When you do this, which of these statements is correct?

- The ruler has fast vibrations and produces a high sound.
- The ruler has slow vibrations and produces a low sound.

What happens to the sound and the speed of the vibrations when you shorten the length of the ruler sticking out over the table?

How high or low a sound is, is called the **pitch**. You can change the pitch of your ruler by changing the length that is vibrating. The vibrations made by a high sound are much closer together and more frequent, so many more vibrations each second reach your ears. We say that a high sound has a high **frequency**. The vibrations made by a low sound are slower and further apart and so fewer vibrations reach your ears each second. We say that a low sound has a low frequency.

Musicians change the pitch of their instruments by changing the speed of the vibrations. This is done in different ways in different instruments.

To do: Tissue box guitar

You will need:

- empty tissue box
- elastic bands of different thicknesses

1. Stretch the elastic bands over the tissue box and pluck them to make a sound.

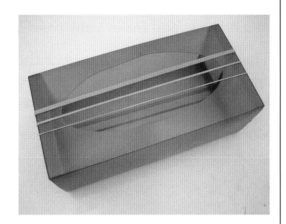

2. Listen carefully to the different sounds made by the thinner and the thicker elastic bands. Arrange the bands on your box in order by putting the higher pitched bands on one side and the lower pitched bands on the other side.

3. Try other ways of changing the pitch of the sound. What happens if you shorten the vibrating part of the elastic band by pressing down on it with your finger in different places? What difference does it make if you stretch the bands more tightly?

When playing your tissue box guitar, you should have found that different elastic bands made different pitched sounds.

The *thinner* and *shorter* bands vibrate more quickly and so give *higher* pitched sounds.

The *thicker* and *longer* bands vibrate more slowly and make *lower* sounds.

A violin has thinner strings to make the higher pitched notes and thicker strings to make the lower notes. Each string can be made to make a higher sound by pressing down on the string with a finger. This has the effect of shortening the string.

The tightness of the string also affects the pitch. You may have seen a violin player tuning the instrument before playing it. Strings can be tightened or loosened by turning the wooden pegs at the end of the neck. The *tighter* the string, the *higher* the pitch of the note.

double bass

cello

violin

Violins, cellos and double basses are the same shape but different sizes so they make different pitched sounds

Now think about the cello and the double bass. They are larger than the violin. They have much thicker and longer strings so they make a range of much lower pitched sounds.

Clarinets, trumpets and recorders do not have strings that can be shortened. Can you remember what vibrates in these instruments?

When we play wind instruments the column of air inside the instrument begins to vibrate. The pitch can be changed by changing the length of the column of vibrating air. If you cover all the holes when you blow through a recorder, the vibrations will have to travel all the way to the opening at the bottom. The column of vibrating air is long and the pitch will be low. If you lift off your fingers as you play, the air can escape through the holes and the pitch becomes higher as the column of vibrating air gets shorter.

To do: Musical straws

You will need:

- plastic straws
- scissors

1. Cut the straws to different lengths.

2. Cut one end of each straw to a point and squeeze it flat.

3. For each straw, put the pointed end in your mouth and blow very hard. Each straw should make a different sound. Will the long straws make a higher or lower sound? What is vibrating in the straw when you blow?

To do: Bottle music

You will need:

- empty bottles (clear glass, all the same size, and with wide necks to help with filling)
- water
- pencil or stick

1. Pour a different amount of water into each of the bottles.

2. Tap the shoulder of the bottles gently with a pencil or stick, and listen to the different sounds.

3. Arrange the bottles in order, with the lower pitched sounds at one end and the higher pitched sounds at the other. You can change the pitch of the notes by adding water or pouring some away.

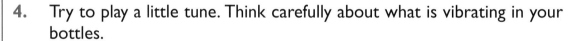

4. Try to play a little tune. Think carefully about what is vibrating in your bottles.

5. Now play your bottles again but this time blow gently across the top of your bottle. What is vibrating now? What do you notice about the pitch of the sounds?

This time it is the air inside the bottle vibrating. The deeper the column of air the lower the pitch will sound.

When you hit the bottles, the glass above the water level begins to vibrate and makes a sound. The lower the water level, the longer the length of glass that can vibrate and so the lower the sound.

Look at a xylophone. Which notes will be higher, the long bars or the shorter bars?

Percussion instruments are played by hitting or shaking them. Many of them can only make one sound but some percussion instruments can make sounds of different pitch.

A xylophone is played by hitting bars made from wood. Each bar is a different length. Which notes will be higher, the long bars or the shorter bars?

The pitch of some drums can be changed by tightening the skin. When the skin is tighter the vibrations will be faster and of a higher frequency so the sound will be higher. A lower sound with a lower frequency can be made by loosening the skin.

Changing volume

The **volume** of a sound is how loud or soft the sound is. The volume of a sound can be changed by making the vibrations bigger or smaller.

Loud sounds make *larger* vibrations. When a drummer bangs a drum really hard, he makes really big vibrations and the big vibrations are carried more easily to our ears.

Soft sounds make *smaller* vibrations. For example, you need to listen carefully when someone whispers.

How does a recorder player or a clarinetist change the volume of the sound when they are playing their instruments? What must a guitar player do to make a loud sound?

Exercise 9.5

Use the words in the box to fill in the gaps in the sentences below. Each word may be used once, more than once or not at all.

| volume air louder vibrates shortened softer pitch |
| high thinner longer higher lower tighter harder thicker |

1. Musical instruments make a sound when something _____ .

2. The _____ is how high or low the sound is.

3. A thin string on a violin will make a higher _____ sound than a thick string.

4. The double bass has _____ and _____ strings than a violin and makes lower sounds.

5. The column of _____ inside the clarinet vibrates.

6. A longer column of air will make a _____ pitched sound.

7. A drum with a _____ skin will make a _____ pitched sound.

8. The _____ of a sound is a measure of how loud it is.

9. To make a louder sound with a drum you need to hit it _____ .

10. To make a _____ sound with a recorder you must blow more gently.

Exercise 9.6

1. Make a list of musical instruments. Sort them into groups according to what is vibrating. Is it the air, strings, reed, skin or something else that vibrates? Make a table in your book and record the instruments in the table. Don't forget to give each column a heading.

2. Explain how you would play a low note on a recorder and what is happening inside the recorder to make a low sound.

3. Describe the differences in the vibrations when a high note is played on a violin and a low note is played on a double bass.

4. Explain how a drummer can change the volume of the sound he makes when he hits the drum.

Exercise 9.7: Extension question

Imagine you have found an old guitar in the attic. The strings are loose and when you pluck the strings they make a horrible sound. Describe how you would adjust the strings in order to make a nicer sound. Try to find out what sound (pitch) each string on a guitar should make. What can help you to tune your guitar strings to make the correct sounds?

Did you know?
Evelyn Glennie is a professional percussion soloist who has been completely deaf from the age of 12. She does not wear shoes when she performs because she feels the vibrations of the music through her feet and other parts of her body. She can detect the pitch of a note depending where on her body she feels the vibrations. She plays familiar percussion instruments but also creates her own by using scrap bits of metal, flower pots and cooking utensils. She might use up to 60 different percussion instruments in a concert. She is a very gifted percussionist who plays with great sensitivity despite her profound deafness.

Chapter 10: More about forces

What is a force?

In *Junior Science Books 1* and *2* we studied two different types of force: magnetic forces and friction. You learnt that magnets can push or pull each other and can pull magnetic materials towards them. Magnets can also be used to stop things moving, for instance when they are used to keep something stuck to the door of your fridge. Friction can slow down moving objects or stop them moving altogether.

A force is a **push**, a **pull** or a **twist** applied to an object.

Forces can:

- start something moving
- slow down or speed up a moving object
- stop a moving object
- change the direction in which an object is moving
- change the shape or size of an object

Can you think of some examples for each of these? The picture below may give you some ideas.

Spotting forces

Forces are around us all the time. Some of them are easy to spot, for example you can see when someone is pushing down on a computer key or pulling a door open. Others, such as friction, cannot be seen so easily.

Have a look at this picture. How many forces can you spot?

Forces diagrams

When scientists record their findings or observations, they often do so in the form of a diagram. We can use diagrams as a way of showing, quickly and simply, how a force is acting on an object. This is done using arrows. The direction of the arrow shows the direction in which the force is acting and the length of the arrow can be used to represent the strength of the force. The tail of the arrow should always be at the place where the force is acting.

Here is an example. We will learn more about the different forces later.

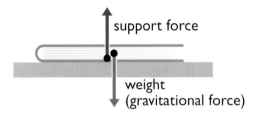

The book rests on the table and the table supports its weight. The downward pull, the gravitational force, is balanced by the upward support force made by the table. The arrows are therefore the same length.

Notice that the arrow showing the weight (gravitational force) starts right in the middle of the book. This spot is called the **centre of gravity** and is where we consider the weight of the object to act.

Did you know?
You can find the exact centre of gravity of an object, by trying to balance it on the point of a pencil. The centre of gravity is found at the place where you can balance the object without it falling off.

Here is another example of a forces diagram.

In this picture, one dog is stronger than the other. Its pulling force is greater so the arrow showing its force is longer. The forces are therefore unbalanced and the winning dog will pull the losing dog across the ground.

Gravity

In the forces diagram on page 156, we saw the action of **gravitational force**. We also saw this force in the picture on page 155, where rocks were falling off the cliff.

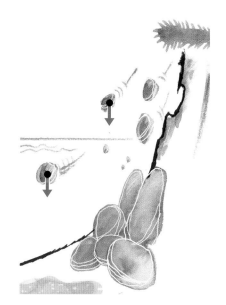

Gravitational force is a rather mysterious force that pulls objects towards each other. The bigger the object, the greater the gravitational force. Earth is a huge object, so it exerts a comparatively large gravitational force pulling everything towards the Earth's centre. This is why, wherever we are in the world, when we drop something, it always falls downwards towards the centre of the Earth.

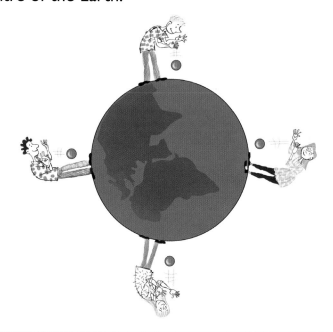

Did you know?
The Moon is about six times smaller than the Earth so its gravitational force is six times smaller. However, the Moon's gravity is strong enough to affect the Earth. It pulls on the water in the sea causing it to pile up more on the side of the Earth facing the Moon. As the Earth rotates and the Moon moves around the Earth, this piling up of the water happens in different places at different times. This effect causes the **tides**.

Exercise 10.1

Use the words in the box to complete the sentences below. Each word may be used once, more than once or not at all.

> speed   push   direction   gravitational   twist   pull   friction
> brakes   force   stop

1. A force is a _____ , a _____ or a _____ that is applied to an object.

2. Forces can change the _____ or _____ of a moving object.

3. _____ is a force that slows down moving objects.

4. Magnets can _____ magnetic materials towards them.

5. The _____ force pulls everything towards the centre of the Earth.

. . . .

Elastic forces

Look at the boy with a catapult in the picture on page 155. Did you think about how a catapult works? You may remember that in *Junior Science Book 2* we learnt about force meters. A force meter has a spring inside it. Force meters should be treated carefully because they can be damaged if too much force is applied. Let's find out a bit more about forces made by things that can be stretched and squeezed.

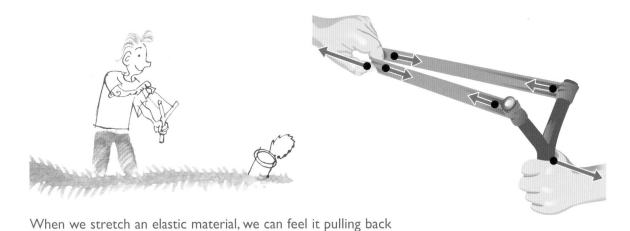

When we stretch an elastic material, we can feel it pulling back

To do: Stretching and squeezing

You will need:

- rubber band
- sponge

1. Loop the rubber band around one finger of each hand. Keep your hands well away from your eyes in case the rubber band snaps or comes off your fingers.

2. Gradually pull your hands away from each other so that you stretch the band. Think about what you can feel. Then move your hands together and take off the rubber band.

   You are using your muscles to pull on the band to stretch it. What is the rubber band doing? You can probably feel it pulling your hands towards each other. It is reacting to the force that you are applying and making its own force in the opposite direction.

3. Now take the sponge and push down on it gently or squeeze it so that you are pushing it inwards in several directions. Think about what you can feel. What will happen when you stop pushing?

The sponge is also reacting to your pushing force. It pushes back to return to its original shape. We often use the word **elastic** as a noun to mean the stretchy tape that is often used in clothing. However, scientists use the word elastic as an adjective to describe materials, like the rubber in the band and the foam in the sponge. They return to their original shape and size after being stretched or squeezed.

See if you can spot other examples of pushes and pulls made by things that have been stretched or squeezed.

Some materials will behave like elastic for a while but then break if they are pulled too much. When this happens we say that they have passed their **elastic limit**. We can do experiments to find the elastic limit of materials.

To do: Find the elastic limit

You will need:

- retort stand and clamp
- spring
- pile of newspapers or a piece of foam
- safety glasses or goggles
- metre ruler
- 100 g mass hanger
- 100 g masses

1. Set up your retort stand with the clamp near the top.

2. Loop your spring over the bar of the clamp. Place the retort stand near the edge of the table so that the spring is hanging over the edge.

3. Put the foam or pile of newspapers on the floor under the spring. You will be hanging a large amount of weight on the spring and this padding will help protect the floor if the apparatus all crashes down. Remember to keep your feet out of the way!

4. Put on your safety glasses or goggles and make sure that you keep them on throughout the experiment. If your spring slips or breaks it could flick up into your face and damage your eyes.

5. Using the metre rules, measure the length of the spring. You will need to decide exactly where on the spring you will measure and then make sure that you measure to the same place at each stage in the experiment. Record your measurement carefully in a table.

6. Hang the 100 g mass hanger carefully on the spring. Wait for it to stop moving up and down, and then measure the length of the spring again and record the new length.

7. Take the mass hanger off and check that the spring returns to its original length. Return the 100 g mass hanger to the spring.

8. Add another 100 g mass to the mass hanger, hang it on the spring and measure and record the new length. Check that the spring returns to its original length when the hanger is removed.

9. Repeat this process, adding one more 100 g mass each time and remembering to check whether the spring returns to its original length.

10. Eventually you will find that when you remove the mass, the spring does not go back to its original length but remains a bit stretched. Make sure that you make a note of when this happens. What mass on the spring caused it to pass its elastic limit?

11. It is quite fun to go on adding more mass to see what happens. Do it carefully, making sure that you keep your face and feet away from the spring as it may suddenly fail and spring back into your face, dropping the masses onto the floor. Measure the spring accurately each time and record the result. You do not need to take the masses off each time now since you know that the elastic limit has been passed.

12. Plot a line graph with 'Mass added, in g' on the horizontal axis and 'Length of spring, in cm' on the vertical axis. What do you notice about the shape of the graph? If you have done your measurements accurately, you should find that it starts off as a straight line. What happens to the line when the elastic limit is reached?

When you have tried this with a spring, you could try the same method to test other elastic materials, such as a rubber band, some elastic tape or maybe something like a jelly sweet in the shape of a loop or some bubblegum.

Reaction forces

When you stretch or squeeze elastic objects you can feel the forces exerted in reaction to the forces made on them. It is easy to feel these forces in something such as a rubber band or a spring but there are other **reaction forces** we take for granted and might not even know are there.

Do you remember the story of Goldilocks and the Three Bears? In the story, Goldilocks tries out the chairs in the bears' house, sitting on each chair in turn. The first two chairs support her, but when she sits on Baby Bear's chair it breaks because she is too heavy for it. Let's think about what happens.

The Earth's gravitational force pulls everything downwards. This force keeps Goldilocks on the ground and stops her from floating away into space. It also makes her push down on any surface that is supporting her. This downward force is called **weight** and is measured in newtons (N). The size of the weight depends on how much of the object there is, its **mass**, which is measured in kilograms, and the size of the gravitational force. You will learn more about this later.

Goldilocks probably has a weight of about 350 N. Daddy Bear, a full grown grizzly bear, may have a weight of about 2500 N and Mummy Bear would have a weight of about 1500 N. Their chairs would be very strong. Baby Bear would be much smaller, maybe with a weight of 300 N.

When Goldilocks sits on Daddy Bear's chair, her weight pushes down on it but she does not fall through. The chair supports her weight. This means that the chair makes a reaction force, pushing upwards to balance the downward force of Goldilocks's weight. Baby Bear's chair is not able to make such a big upward force. Goldilocks's weight is too much for it, so it breaks.

This upward force is exerted every time an object is placed on a surface. It is sometimes called a reaction force but is also known as the **support force**. (Look back at the forces diagram on page 156). Some surfaces can exert large support forces; some can only exert small ones. For example, even the heaviest person can walk on a pavement without falling through, but soft mud is unable to support our weight very well, and no one can walk on water.

Exercise 10.2

1. What do scientists mean when they use the word 'elastic'?

2. Explain clearly why it is important not to pull the spring in a force meter too strongly. Use the term 'elastic limit' in your answer, making it clear what this means.

3. (a) Explain why a book that is placed on a table does not fall through it.

   (b) Explain in terms of support forces, why it is dangerous to walk on ice on a pond.

Upthrust

Take another look at the picture on page 155. Notice the boats in the picture. Did you explain what forces were making them move along? You probably did, but did you also explain what force was holding them up in the water? If not, you should now be able to explain this using your knowledge of support forces.

Water exerts a support force that has a special name, it is called **upthrust**. The gravitational force pulls the boat downwards but is matched by the upthrust of the water pushing upwards on the bottom of the boat. Of course, if the boat gets too heavy, the water can no longer support its weight and the boat will sink.

To do: Weighing in water

You will need:

- a variety of objects (these will get wet so choose ones that will not be damaged by water)
- string or a netting bag to put the objects in
- force meter
- bowl of water

1. Draw a table, like the one below, to record your results.

Object	Weight, in N	Reading in water, in N	Does the object float or sink?

2. Start by hanging one of the objects from the force meter, using the string or netting bag to attach it to the hook on the force meter. You are measuring the weight of the object in newtons. Record this weight carefully in the table.

3. Now lower each object carefully onto the water. Do not let the object touch the bottom of the bowl. Look carefully at the reading on the force meter and record it carefully in the table.

4. Repeat this with the other objects, recording your results each time.

5. Now put all the objects into the water and record whether they float or sink.

6. Look at your results. What do you notice? Is there any pattern? Can you explain what is happening? What happened to the reading when something that floated was put into the water?

When an object is put into water, the upthrust works against the gravitational force. If the object floats, the two forces exactly balance one another. The gravitational force is cancelled out by the upthrust, so the reading on the force meter in the experiment will be zero. If the object is too heavy, the upthrust cannot cancel the gravitational force entirely so the object sinks. The reading on the force meter will not be zero but it will always be less than the reading taken when the object is not in the water.

Exercise 10.3

1. What name is given to the support force made by water?

2. Look at the canoe in the picture on page 155. Explain, in terms of forces, how it floats.

3. The human body floats naturally. When people first started to spend more than a few minutes under the water, they wore diving suits with heavy boots. Explain how this helped them.

Early divers needed boots weighted with lead

Exercise 10.4: Extension question

A steel nail will sink if put into water. A huge ship made from steel floats easily. Suggest an explanation for this.

To do: Draw forces arrows

You will need:

- pictures showing forces acting on objects (you could draw these, cut them from newspapers or magazines or maybe your teacher will give you some)

- ruler   • pencil or coloured pencils

Look carefully at each picture and identify the forces acting on the object. Think about whether the forces are balanced (the forces are equal) or unbalanced (the forces are unequal). If they are unbalanced think about which force is bigger.

Use your ruler and pencils to draw arrows on the pictures to show the forces acting. Remember to make the length of the arrow show the relative strength of the forces.

Exercise 10.5

Use the words in the box to complete the following sentences. Each word may be used once, more than once or not at all.

centre of gravity   unbalanced   shorter   length   point   arrows
longer   balanced   tail   direction   upthrust   mass

1. Forces can be shown on diagrams using _____ .

2. The direction in which the force is acting is shown by the _____ of the arrow.

3. The relative strength of the forces is shown by the _____ of the arrow.

4. If the forces are _____ , the arrows will be the same length.

5. If the forces are unbalanced, the stronger force is shown by a _____ arrow.

6. The _____ of the arrow should be at the point where the force is acting.

7. The gravitational force is considered to act at the _____ .

· ·

Index

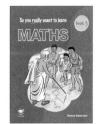

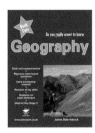

Galore Park
JUNIOR SERIES

GALORE PARK

- Perfect for working towards Key Stage 2 and Common Entrance at 11+

- Suitable for the specialist or non specialist teacher or parent

- Rigorous, challenging material to stretch pupils

- Clear explanations and worked examples

- Plenty of exercises to ensure pupils have understood each topic

- Answer books also available

- Full of practical activities and interesting facts